Cinemas in Britain

One Hundred Years of Cinema Architecture

Richard Gray

Lund Humphries Publishers, London

Produced in collaboration
with the Cinema Theatre Association

Cinemas in Britain

First published in 1996 by
Lund Humphries Publishers
Park House
1 Russell Gardens
London NW11 9NN

Produced in collaboration with the Cinema Theatre Association

ISBN 0 85331 685 6

British Library Cataloguing in Publication Data
A catalogue record of this book is available from the British Library.

Distributed in the USA by
Antique Collectors' Club
Market Street Industrial Park
Wappingers Falls
NY 12590
USA

Designed by Ray Carpenter
Typeset by Nene Phototypesetters, Northampton
Made and printed in Belgium by Snoeck Ducaju & Zoon N.V.

Photographic Credits

The author and publishers thank the following for providing photographs.

Every effort has been made to trace the copyright holders of photographs. If any institutions or individuals have been incorrectly credited, or if there are any omissions, we would be glad to be notified so that the necessary corrections can be made in any reprint.

Contents

Acknowledgements

The genesis of this book lies in a letter I wrote to Jill Lever, former curator of the RIBA Drawings Collection, during 1993, suggesting that the centenary of cinema would be an opportune moment to mount an exhibition on cinema architecture. To my great joy Mrs Lever readily accepted the idea and the exhibition opened three years later at the RIBA Heinz Gallery, two days after the actual anniversary of the Lumières' first film presentation on 20 February. The book grew out of the exhibition and I have to thank Carol Gibbons, patron of the Cinema Theatre Association, who provided very generous sponsorship for both projects.

I have to thank the members of the Cinema Theatre Association committee who have provided support and encouragement, but particularly the Honorary Secretary of the Association, Adam Unger, who contributed his extensive knowledge of the New Victoria cinema and its architect Ernest Wamsley Lewis, and helped with the picture research. Other members of the committee — Allen Eyles, David Trevor-Jones, Elain Harwood, Jeremy Buck and Tony Moss — have kindly read the typescript, contributed extra information and made helpful suggestions. Allen Eyles also let me use photographs from his collection. I have to thank Brian Oakaby, the Cinema Theatre Association archivist, for allowing me to ransack his archive and retain material for many months. Help has also been provided by: Kevin Wheelan, who provided images from his vast photographic collection; Jean William, David Eve and Gary Trinder for information and a photograph of the Central Hall cinema, Colne, Lancashire; Bruce Peter for help with Scottish cinemas; Keith Skone and John Skinner on cinemas in Wales; Peter Jones, Keith Tricker, Richard Cole and David Wilmore on projection, the earliest years of film, mechanical musical instruments and theatre lighting respectively; and Frank Mander for information on John Alexander.

Public bodies and archives have responded speedily such as CADW (Edward Holland); Heritage Scotland (Roddy McDougall); the Worcestershire County Archivists Office; Colne Public Library; and the British Film Institute Stills Collection.

Finally, I must thank Jeffery West and Glyn Coppack of English Heritage for their interest and encouragement in both projects; Geoffrey Smith-Wyatt for volunteering to type the first part of the manuscript; Audrey Hannan (formerly of English Heritage) who helped with correspondence and finally cured me of 'techno-phobia', gently introducing me to the world of the word processor; and my long-suffering editor at Lund Humphries.

Richard Gray May 1996

Introduction: Early Memories

This book is inspired by the excitement, magic and mystery of cinema and theatre buildings. I fell in love with them at an early age and they have always held an extraordinary fascination for me. I think my earliest recollection was of being taken at a very young age, only perhaps five or six years old, to a performance at the Streatham Hill Theatre in south London. What was happening on stage was of no interest to me. I distinctly remember turning round in my front stalls seat to gaze in wonderment at the auditorium – vast and dark with rising galleries and a sea of faces looking over my head at the stage and its goings-on. I am sure I remember this but, of course, very early memories become confused with what I might have been told happened for, no doubt, this behaviour must have been extremely irritating for my mother and grandfather who had gone to all that trouble to take me to a Christmas 'panto'. Unfortunately, neither are around now to check the authenticity of the story.

In fact, my mother was nearly born in a cinema according to a story recalled by her younger sister. My mother's parents, together with my great-aunt, had a regular film date together at another Streatham palace of entertainment, the Golden Domes cinema.

Towards the end of the show my pregnant grandmother felt that Sylvia, my mother, was on the way, and the whole party left post haste in a taxi for their home in nearby West Norwood, where Sylvia appeared later that night, just a week before Christmas, 1914.

Like countless other London children, I had a Christmas treat to see *Peter Pan* at the now disappeared Scala Theatre in Charlotte Street, an oddly located building on the edge of Bloomsbury, well away from the West End proper. I was a lucky little only child, always ushered into the most desirable parts of an auditorium, perhaps not the top price seats, but certainly the stalls or dress circle. The Scala was, like so many London theatres, constructed like an iceberg, with almost more of it below ground than above the surface. This makes access much easier, taking you down one storey to reach the main floor and only rising one or two levels to reach the upper balconies. The fortunate dress circle patrons have no stairs to climb and this esoteric feature of theatre architecture I still find intriguing. It struck me then as extraordinary and I wondered why the building was so. It does at least indicate a precocious appreciation of theatre planning, when other children were more absorbed by Tinkerbell and Captain Hook!

Introduction

We moved to Croydon, which, as far as entertainment was concerned, was dominated by the Davis, built as a super cinema but always referred to locally as the Davis 'Theatre'. I think there was a feeling that the name 'cinema' was inadequate for this massive and palatial structure and that, as it frequently presented shows other than films, it should be accorded the dignity of being referred to as a 'theatre'. In the late 1950s, cinemas were absolutely part of everyday life — they stood sentinel on street corners as though they had been there for all time. The cinema was as constant as the church, school or swimming pool. Timeless though the Davis may have appeared, it had in fact little time to go, and was demolished in 1959, only thirty-one years after opening. It is salutary to consider that it has now been gone for more years than it was in existence. It was there that I made the acquaintance of the voice of the cinema, the generically termed Wurlitzer organ (although a different brand in the Davis), from a seat a thousand miles back at the rear of the upper balcony, high up amongst art-deco electroliers, on a school trip to see a film of the Bolshoi Ballet (actually filmed on the Davis's stage). But what on earth was this, after the curtains had finally closed, a great white monster in a spotlight was rising from the depths of the orchestra pit? I craned forward with rapt attention in my distant seat, transfixed until it sank into oblivion, but I kept my exhilaration to myself.

A red double-decker bus links this part of mundane south London with another, Tooting, which had and — glory to behold — still has, the Granada cinema at its centre. It was worth the short bus ride over Mitcham Common to visit this ultimate 'Cathedral of the Movies', certainly a suitable appellation for the rampantly Gothic interior. Despite the fact that Saturday afternoon audiences in the mid-1960s appeared to consist of only a handful of people — the fullest I ever saw it was for a Wurlitzer concert by Reginald Foort — it never occurred to me that this mighty concern could actually close, but surely it did, in 1973, and bingo took over a few years later. But back in 1964 I regularly mounted the shallow steps up to the entrance doors, grasped an antiqued iron door handle on a stained oak door, pushed against its daunting weight and addressed the paybox cowering under stagey Gothic cusping. Ethereal Mantovani echoed from the foyer as I grabbed my change, impatient to get in. An acre of travertine to traverse, ingesting the 'Baronial Gothic' foyer; on through the infinite reflections of the inner lobby, all plate glass and gold columns; a glance at Le Blond's sketches of troubadours for the murals on the auditorium walls, and at last into the great cavernous 'cathedral', to a seat under the balcony, not too far forward, not too far back. Was the balcony ever open? Were there other living souls? No, just widely spaced heads

Davis, Croydon, Surrey, 1928

attending the screen in the inky blackness — dream-like, like a sequence from a surrealist film. Then the interminable wait until the film credits rolled, the curtains swung across the final image, their thickness muffling the sound-track, and the 'cathedral' awoke with a thousand Gothic niches set aglow by countless tiny light bulbs, the slave of a master dimmer switch behind the scenes. Sometimes I would plunge through a quatrefoiled emergency exit door to marvel at the sheer scale of the building (hemmed in by late Victorian terraces) and ponder at the curious way the rear jutted out over the car park as though it was about to outgrow its site. The Granada is still there, but the auditorium is now lit from above in order for bingo players to scrutinise their game cards accurately.

Nostalgic this all may seem, but it is surely more than that: a realisation that these buildings were and, where they survive, are special and important. Official approbation came for the 'cathedral' in 1972 when it was one of the first cinemas to be listed. Until that time, cinema buildings had not been taken seriously, only viewed through nostalgia's eyes. Architectural historians had not given a second glance to a cinema; indeed, they were only just beginning to accept the works of Phipps and Matcham from the previous era of the music hall.

1: The Moving Image: Invention and Pioneers

The origins of film as a medium lie in two spheres of activity which were taking place in the mid-nineteenth century. One of these was the invention of photography in France and Britain during the 1830s, and the other was the magic lantern show, a presentation of painted projected slides which came to include photographs. There were also the great panorama shows of huge mobile painted screens such as the Dioramas in Regent's Park and Leicester Square in London, but these metropolitan attractions were too expensive to be constructed in large numbers. The magic lantern show had the advantage of being portable and could be set up in any room quickly and easily; one can imagine the apparatus being erected in the larger rooms of coaching inns across Britain.

The tremendous success of the live music hall from the middle of the century eclipsed the static visual image as a public attraction. But, like the longing for flight, the invention of the moving picture was perceived as one of the crowning ambitions of man, and serious scientific research was taking place at the time into the very nature of movement. In the USA in the 1870s Eadweard Muybridge was investigating motion with the aid of a series of rapid-action cameras arranged along a horizontal fence-like structure. This produced a

sequence of photographs revealing how man walked or ran. He also tried the same experiment with a galloping horse to discover whether all four legs ever lift off the ground simultaneously. For a split second they did! But this was a strip of photographs, not animation. The vital elements required to transform the static into the moving image were the invention of a flexible film substance through which light could be shone – celluloid; a sensitive coating for that film fast enough to capture an image in a fraction of a second; an intense light source, which already existed in the form of limelight (later, carbon arc light) – the theatre spotlight; and a camera mechanism which could be duplicated in the projector, whereby the film could be advanced with the aid of perforations or sprockets. The advancing but momentarily static film frame exploited the principle of the persistence of retinal image, in which our eyes (and in the signal transmitted to the brain) perceive a series of images, when revealed with great rapidity, as a single moving picture. The revolving Victorian children's toy, the zoetrope, demonstrates this same principle. The camera projection mechanism was the most technically difficult obstacle to overcome. The story of the technology which led to the aforesaid elements being combined into a practical system is not the subject of this book, but a number of inventors were working on it including Max and Emil Skladanowsky in Germany, Robert Paul and Birt Acres in England, the Lumière brothers in France, and Thomas Edison in the USA.

Initially of greatest significance were the inventions patented as the 'Kinetograph' (the camera) and the 'Kinetoscope' (the viewing machine) by Thomas Edison in the USA in 1890. The work was actually accomplished by his assistant, William Dickson, and consisted of all the components mentioned earlier, but relied on an ordinary electric light bulb, rather than the strong light source. The viewing machine resembled a peep-show, similar to the 'Mutascope' or 'What the Butler Saw' machines once to be found in pier arcades. The first Kinetoscope parlour opened in Chicago in 1894, followed by several others in New York and elsewhere in the USA. The first London Kinetoscope parlour opened on 17 October of the same year, at 70 Oxford Street. Initially, the public paid admission at the door, but later entrance was free, with the viewing machines operated on the coin-in-the-slot principle. Reconstructions of these ingenious machines can be seen today in the Museum of the Moving Image in London. Movement was of the essence in these films, lasting, as they did, for only about thirty seconds. They typically featured displays of exotic dancing or the action of a blacksmith's shop, so transient was the entertainment.

The Kinetograph (the camera) was a closely guarded secret, and the films it produced were protected by American copyright laws. Robert Paul, an electrical engineer and scientific instrument maker in Hatton Garden, London, had been active in successfully manufacturing copies of Kinetoscopes, which were not protected by patents in Britain. Until then, only the Edison Company had been able to supply the films, and Paul realised that in order to encourage future sales of the viewing machines, a more dependable supply of films would be needed. To this end, he and his collaborator Birt Acres set about constructing a home-grown camera to provide the supply. This achieved, the partnership dissolved due to a disagreement over the patent of the camera and the two became rivals in the ultimate race to exhibit projected film. Although it was Paul who had had the genesis of the idea of film projection in the summer of 1895, he did nothing until news of the Lumière brothers' success in Paris, and their intention to repeat it in London, spurred him into action. However, Acres pipped him to the post, demonstrating his 'Kinetic Lantern' to the Royal Photographic Society on 14 January 1896. Paul's 'Theatrograph' performance for the Finsbury Technical College coincided to the day with the Lumières' London premiere in February of the same year.

Auguste and Louis Lumière had given the first public perform-

ance of their 'Kinétoscope de Projection' (later renamed the Cinématographe) in the basement of a café near the Paris Opéra on 28 December 1895. This seems to have been a success and the Lumières patented the process. On 20 February 1896 the Lumières' system was shown to an audience of the press and invited guests in the Great Hall of the old Regent Street Polytechnic Institution in London. The Lumière brothers, who were busy running a photographic plate-making business near Paris, sent a collaborator, Félicien Trewey or Treuwé, a conjuror and shadow-graph artist, to organise the London presentation. The audience was dazzled by scenes of family life, people bathing in the Mediterranean, and most alarming of all, a steam train pulling into a station and disgorging its passengers. For the London opening Trewey hired a room in an educational institution, where the films would certainly be taken seriously. It was not long, however, before the gaudy and glamorous world of the music hall, then almost at the peak of its popularity, embraced the new medium. Trewey had intended to hire the Polytechnic hall for three months, but an offer from the management of the Empire theatre, Leicester Square, curtailed the programme at that theatre from 9 March. The Lumières were talented publicists — a film was shot of the exterior of the Empire with a huge banner draped across its entrance announcing the 'Cinématographe'. This film was then shown to the audience inside, so that they could experience the heightened reality of viewing a moving picture of the exterior of the very theatre in which they were sitting, showing all the passing street life. Little did the management of the Empire, possibly the most famous music hall in Britain, realise that it was introducing a cuckoo, which after growing to stupendous proportions would, in a little over thirty years, cause the demise of that very theatre to make way for one of London's most opulent movie palaces. The Polytechnic building (now the University of Westminster headquarters) has since been reconstructed, but the envelope walls of the Great Hall survive, as do some of the original roof timbers hidden above the fibrous plaster ceiling, installed when the hall was remodelled as a full-time cinema in 1927.

The Lumières aside, the rivalry between Birt Acres and Robert Paul continued. Acres presented his newly named 'Kineopticon' on 21 March 1896 at 2 Piccadilly Mansions, at the corner of Piccadilly Circus and Shaftesbury Avenue. Paul, after demonstrating his 'Theatrograph' at the Olympia exhibition hall on 19 March, hired the Egyptian Hall, Piccadilly, but was lured away to another Leicester Square theatre, the Alhambra, on 25 March, renaming his film system the 'Animatograph'. The movies had taken Leicester

Programme from the Lumières'
film show at the Regent Street
Polytechnic, London, in 1896

Great Hall of the Regent Street Polytechnic,
London, in c.1896

The old Empire, Leicester Square,
London, in 1896

Square by storm, where they still reign to this day. The Alhambra theatre, originally built in 1852 as the Royal Panoption of Arts and Sciences, a failed quasi-scientific attraction, was later re-constructed as a conventional Victorian theatre. It was demolished in 1936, and the Odeon now stands on the site.

Birt Acres's Kineoptikon is of greatest importance, however, as his premises on Piccadilly Circus might be termed the first British cinema. While it may only have been a temporary conversion from retail purposes, it was specifically dedicated to the exhibition of films, not as a part of a music hall programme or in a location more akin to a scientific experiment such as the Polytechnic Institution. The leasing of this shop announced the commercial future of the movies – as high profile entertainment sited in a central location, easy to find, with abundant passing trade. The premises have returned to retail use after long occupation as the Eros Newsreel theatre.

In no time at all, the Lumières' projector was copied. A projector manufactured by Léon Gaumont appeared in the same year, and the machines soon became readily available. The projectors were very small, making them easy to transport. Immediately shows were presented in theatres and halls nationwide. Possibly the first showing outside London was at the Pandora Gallery, Kings Road, Brighton, on the same day as Robert Paul's presentation at the Alhambra, on 25 March.

Thereafter, different protagonists took film to the four corners of Britain either as a 'turn' at the local music hall or by hiring premises, like the YMCA in Manchester on 4 May 1896, or on 26 of the same month, the Real Ice Skating Palace in Glasgow. Even the Public Baths in Walsall were pressed into service in November of the same year. Royal approval of the new medium came when the Lumières presented films to Queen Victoria at Windsor Castle in 1897. Early film presentations were often accompanied by an announcer who stood by the screen and provided a commentary on each scene, rather like a lecturer. The important development away from this rather forced procedure, which must have been difficult to hear against the clatter of the projector mechanism, was the realisation that film could tell its own story without explanation. The earliest films were of a documentary nature which captured the simple movement of the real world – a novelty in itself at the time. A camera mounted on the front of a railway locomotive proved a great diversion, but promoters quickly realised the infinitely greater capabilities of the new medium.

Forever quick on the uptake to find some new attraction, films were taken up by travelling fairs. In some respects this was un-fortunate, as their garish presentation coupled with their very

impermanence tended to take the public perception of the cinema away from serious photographic innovation, scientific experiment and 'actualité', which had been the earnest ambition of the cinematograph pioneers. The medium travelled easily from show-ground to country-town market place. A canvas structure would be rigged up with a projector at one end, a white sheet at the other, and rows of benches in between; the whole thing would be fronted by a gaudy, eye-catching façade decorated in fairground style, stand-ing on the steps of which would be the 'barker' encouraging the gullible to venture inside. Very often the short film programmes would be supported by stage acts performed by small dance troupes. Some of these mobile auditoria were very ambitious, accommodat-ing up to 1000 people (although no doubt somewhat squashed together) and with elaborate gilded stage prosceniums matching the exterior. At night, the fairground biograph would be a mass of electric light bulbs, powered by a vast steam traction engine that would also propel the whole show from town to town. In the early days projectors were hand-cranked with limelight providing the source of illumination.

The fairground served to popularise film between its embryonic days and the first generation of permanent cinemas in the early 1900s. In fact, the fairground side-show façade may have had a formative effect on early cinema architectural style – a gaudy show front attached to a shed-like auditorium. The fairground cinema was particularly successful in rural areas such as East Anglia; the Thurston family's travelling bioscope show travelled around Norfolk and Suffolk until the outbreak of the First World War, by which time they had moved into operating purpose-built cinemas. Greens of Glasgow, a well-known Scottish cinema operator of the 1920s and 1930s, also started this way. The ease with which a film show could be established encouraged other early exhibitors to take to the road and set up in any available hall. There were even open-air shows in summer, despite the unreliable English climate.

In 1906 Hale's 'Tours' appeared in England, an extraordinary enterprise imported from the USA, in which travelogue films were projected in a mock railway coach (which was even made to sway like a real train), giving the viewer the impression of being taken on a ten-minute scenic ride through the Rocky Mountains of America or the Swiss Alps, complete with a uniformed ticket collector to wave a flag and blow a whistle. The idea was franchised and 'Tours' (such as Hamilton's Express, in which the world flashed past its windows, all for sixpence) appeared in a number of cities in Britain, the shows in London and Nottingham surviving as late as 1912.

In country towns a favourite place to set up a travelling film show was the corn exchange, an ideal location, invariably in a prominent position on the market place. As we will see in the next chapter, such venues often became permanent cinemas. Elsewhere, municipal or public halls of all types were pressed into service, such as the Great Hall, Tunbridge Wells, and the Assembly Rooms in Bath. The former remained a cinema until the 1950s, but the latter was bombed in the Second World War and later restored as a museum. Among travelling film shows were Ralph Pringle's quaintly named North American Picture Company, A.J. West's Animated Photographs and the St Louis Animated Picture Company – all British concerns, despite the transatlantic sounding names.

A travelling fairground filmshow,
early 1900s

The temporary film show location sometimes evolved into a permanent cinema. This happened with a number of the country corn exchanges, such as the cinema at East Dereham in Norfolk, with its quaint projection box mounted on the otherwise almost unaltered nineteenth-century façade. Another example is at Northampton, where the brick shell of the Victorian corn exchange survives, in which a cinema auditorium was created in 1920. But most noteworthy amongst this type of conversion is the Picture Playhouse in the market place of Beverley, near Hull, which has been open as a cinema since 1911, the only alteration from the building's original purpose as a corn exchange being the stadium-style balcony inserted at the entrance end of the auditorium.

In time, all sorts of unlikely buildings were adapted for the movies, from a former workhouse in Upton Park, east London, where the courtyard was roofed over to form an immense auditorium, to a chapel in Tolmers Square near Euston Station. In the early years of this century, roller-skating became a popular pastime, but when the fashion waned the rinks were easily converted into cinemas. The first Westover cinema, facing the pier at Bournemouth, is an interesting example, as films were shown while the

building was still in operation for roller skating, although it would be difficult to imagine how anyone could watch the film while still rolling around the rink! There is also the still extant Dome Cinema, in another south-coast resort, Worthing. This Edwardian entertainment complex, the Kursaal, dating from 1911, had a ground-floor skating rink, and films were shown, almost as an afterthought, in a room above the foyer. The popularity of the new medium soon killed off skating and the movies were moved down to the larger ground-floor area.

The most convenient structures to convert permanently for cinema use were shop premises, and many such conversions started to appear in the early years of the century. Most of them disappeared, however, with the coming of the 1909 Cinematograph Act, and they are now very difficult to trace and do not often survive in photographs. The shop front would be decked out with hoardings and billboards for the films, with the name of the cinema displayed above the entrance, replacing the old shop fascia. Such cinemas were invariably simply named 'Cinematograph Theatre' (the last 'e' in the Lumières' Cinematographe was quickly dropped), but 'Electric' became popular to emphasise the modernity of the medium.

The Playhouse, Beverley, East Yorkshire, in use as a cinema since 1911

Meanwhile, films had become very much a part of music-hall programmes, and new theatres designed by Frank Matcham and his followers invariably included a projection room on the plans. Legitimate theatres and music halls were also beginning to be converted permanently into cinemas. The Theatre Royal, Attercliffe, Sheffield (demolished in 1961), is recorded as being 'open for cinematographic performances' in 1904, surely one of the first at this early date. However, it is very likely this could allude to intermittent film use only. A season of films was presented in around 1908 at the New Theatre (now the Albery Theatre), St Martin's Lane, London, then only four years old, indicating the pressure from exhibitors to find available auditoria for the movies. Many of the theatres in the West End have at some time housed films, one of the earliest to be converted in 1910 being the long since lost Terry's Theatre in the Strand. However, in suburban London as early as 1907, the Balham Empire became a full-time cinema. It was renamed the 'Theatre de Luxe' for its new life with movies. It stayed open as a cinema until 1960 and was finally demolished in 1974.

A shop conversion to a cinema – the Nelson Electric Theatre, Old Kent Road, London.
Very few photographs of such cinemas survive, and although this photograph was taken in c.1931, it does give a clear idea of what these cinemas were like

'The Dome', Worthing.

The Kursaal, Worthing, West Sussex, 1911.
This cinema was renamed 'The Dome' during the First World War, after a competition was held in Worthing to find a new name to replace the then unpopular German name 'Kursaal'

Montagu Pyke's Edgware
Road Cinematograph
Theatre, north London,
1909

What is accepted as one of the first purpose-built cinemas in Britain still stands today in Colne, Lancashire. Plans were submitted to the local authority on behalf of Joshua Duckworth for a building on Colne Lane and approved in January 1905. Joshua Duckworth was a magic lantern showman and entrepreneur who also ran a firm of printers and stationers. In an article he wrote dated 20 July 1908 for the *Kinematograph and Lantern Weekly* he states that the first saw 'living pictures' on an Edison Kinetoscope and was so impressed with the experience that he bought one of the machines. Being the only one in the Colne area, it was a great novelty and attraction. When projected film made the Kinetoscope obsolete he acquired a Macguire and Baucus Bioscope projector and toured the district with short film programmes supplemented by lantern slides and 'illustrated songs'. This proved popular until the area had been 'worked over and over again', the problem being that he had to actually purchase the films rather than rent them. Soon, however, it was possible to hire the product and, as Duckworth already owned a site in Colne, he decided to build the cinema known as the Central Hall at a cost of £2000. For this he purchased a Gaumont Pro-fessional Chrono projector which he later wrote 'had run every

night [that the cinema was open] for two hours, for nearly two years without giving trouble'. The first recorded press advertisement for this cinema is in February 1907, and this has been accepted as the date of opening. However, as Duckworth was writing in the summer of 1908 that his Gaumont projector had been running for nearly two years, this takes its installation back to the middle of 1906. Clearly, the Central Hall was in operation by this year. Joshua Duckworth died in 1925 and the Central Hall was closed and put up for sale in 1927. It became an engineering training workshop and is now a clothing factory. The building is unlisted and is architecturally un-remarkable, but as one of Britain's oldest purpose-built cinemas its sociological and historical credentials are more than adequate testa-ment to its importance. David Atwell in *Cathedrals of the Movies* cites an earlier example of a purpose-built cinema, the Electric Theatre, Stourport-on-Severn, said to have been constructed in 1904.

What constitutes a purpose-built cinema? A definition would be any auditorium built for film exhibition purposes which is not a conversion of an existing structure. I would qualify this definition by emphasising the word 'auditorium', thereby including cinemas which have their entry through a pre-existing building.

Central Hall, Colne, Lancashire, c.1906

An ambitious early (although strictly speaking, not purpose-built) cinema was the Gem, facing the promenade at Great Yarmouth, Norfolk. As extensively detailed in Stephen Peart's *The Picture House in East Anglia*, there was much speculation in the town during 1908 as to the intended purpose of the building going up on the sea-front. The original intention had been to exhibit wild animals in the new building, but an outcry from the occupiers of the neighbouring properties, many of them seaside boarding houses, about the possible smell (which would be particularly obnoxious during the busy summer season) put paid to the promoters' plans. The scheme was the brainchild of Frank Bostock, an animal exhibitor, and the young Charles Blake Cochran, later to achieve fame as a producer of West End revues. With the animal show thwarted, Bostock and Cochran switched to the latest craze, movies, and the Gem cinema opened on 4 July 1908. The architect was Arthur S. Hewitt, and presumably the building had already been designed in some detail before the plans for its intended use changed, therefore it is difficult to cite it as the first purpose-built cinema still operational. The faience façade of the Gem is typical of entertainment architecture of the time: exuberantly detailed with fashionable baroque features, fruity mouldings surrounding 'œil-de-bœuf' windows; a cathedral-like composition, with twin towers surmounted by fish-scale slate cupolas. The entrance was through a great welcoming porch now fronted by later brick extensions. Internally there was a long narrow hall measuring 140 feet by 42 feet wide. The cinema opened in a great hurry with the scaffolding still up and without the required licence for the musical accompaniment. Between the films there were recitals by the 'Aerophone', a specially constructed instrument which, it was confidently stated, 'could emulate the great singers of the day'. A great attraction was the façade illuminated at night by 1500 bulbs, although Bostock and Cochran advertised the Gem as 'The Palace of 5000 Lights'. It must have looked magical to Edwardian holidaymakers from gas-lit Midlands industrial towns. The auditorium had windows to provide a change of air, but the glass was opaque to exclude most of the light. The best and most luxurious seats were at the front near the screen, like in a theatre or music hall, as it had not occurred to the promoters that the optimum viewing position for the movies was from further back. The programmes lasted for about forty-five minutes and were continuous from eleven o'clock in the morning for twelve hours – there was a sign above the entrance announcing 'Come in when you like and stay as long as you like'. The Gem was a tremendous success, with 17,000 people attending in the first five days, encouraged by Charles Cochran 'barking' at the promenade crowds, in fairground side-show style. Early reports suggest that there were segregated seating areas, as it was considered improper for the sexes to sit together in the dark! The Gem later changed its name to the Windmill and continues today, divided into the 'Odditorium' – an ironical return to the world of the fairground freakshow – with a tiny 140-seat studio cinema in the former balcony. Although not in continuous operation since 1908, the Gem is the oldest functioning cinema in Britain.

Another cinema building dating from this early period is the Dara, Delancey Street in Camden Town, London. Built as a public hall in the 1880s, it became a skating rink in 1903 and then, in 1908, when the skating craze waned, it was largely reconstructed for films. The original paybox is a particularly interesting survival, although the cinema has been closed since the First World War. Not far away, at 75 Upper Street, Islington, in north London, is the remains of another early cinema, the Electric. The most distinguishing feature of this building is a dome surmounted by a female figure (who originally held aloft an electric globe above her head) indicating the former entrance, which was built, like the adjoining shops, in the front garden of a Georgian house. The long, narrow auditorium must have run back at the rear of the house. The promoters were Electric Theatres Ltd. They had planned to open the Electric on Boxing Day 1908, but had to postpone the opening to 6 February 1909. Chris Draper, in his book on Islington cinemas, mentions that the choice of film for the 1909 Christmas season, *The Birth of Christ*, turned out to be controversial,

Gem, Great Yarmouth, Norfolk, 1908

a letter in the *Kinematograph and Lantern Weekly* considering it blasphemous. Film censorship, which began in 1912, banned representations of Christ, as well as any criticism of the monarchy, potentially pornographic scenes and incitements to class hatred.

Being a populous district, Islington had a large number of cinemas, each new wave of construction edging the existing ones, perhaps only in operation a very few years, out of business. The Electric continued until 1916, when competition from the almost adjacent Empress cinema (in recent years renamed the Screen on the Green) and the nearby Angel Picture Theatre forced it to close. It is amazing that the entrance fore-building has survived both structurally and decoratively to give an idea of what a pre-1910 cinema frontage was like. The building is listed Grade II and is now an antiques shop. It would be good to see the illuminated globe restored to working order. Also in north London was Pyke's Finsbury Park Cinematograph Theatre, dating from October 1909. This enterprise could claim to be one of the earliest purpose-built cinemas in London. The immense adjacent skating rink, and former tram-car depot, also became a cinema and Pyke's survived merely as its foyer.

The search for the earliest generation of cinemas is now so often a matter of archaeology. The Casino de Paris cinema of 1909, for instance, in Oxford Street, London, is possibly only represented by a single pilaster (which might have formed one side of the entrance) on the outside of an otherwise entirely non-cinematic late-Victorian commercial building. The New Egyptian Hall cinema of 1907 in Piccadilly, can only be guessed at when standing in an expensive luggage emporium, while the 1909 Circle in the Square cinema in Leicester Square, is commemorated only by a tiny, but extra-ordinarily sharply angled pediment over a pub entrance. All of these cinemas were adaptions from existing premises; the original building survives although the temporary use has long since dis-appeared. What used to be one of the best known of these early cinemas, largely because it boldly advertised that it was the oldest cinema in the country on an exterior wall, was the Electric Theatre or the Biograph in Wilton Road, opposite London's Victoria Station. It claimed to have opened in 1905, but in fact it did not appear until four years later and was almost entirely reconstructed in 1927. The Biograph was demolished in 1983 and the site is still a car park.

Montagu Pyke's Cinematograph
Theatre, Finsbury Park, north London,
1909

4: The Cinematograph Act: The Cinema Building Grows Up

Of seminal importance to the history of the development of cinema buildings is the Cinematograph Act of 1909, which came into force on 1 January 1910. The need for the Act arose out of government and public concern about the fire risk posed by the highly volatile nitrate-based celluloid film. Not only could the film be spontaneously combustible if it was in any state of decomposition, but it could also ignite if it became jammed in the projector light beam aperture (the projector 'gate'). The light source was a naked carbon arc flame (the successor to limelight), which although concealed in its lamp house, also presented a potential fire risk. Realising the danger, early projectionists often rigged up a water tank above the machine to douse the first sign of smouldering celluloid. Projectors were sometimes lethally situated in the middle of the audience, and inevitably there were some dangerous blazes. The early London exhibitor, Montagu Pyke, recounts in an autobiographical article how some waste film ignited while being packed into boxes in the basement of one of his cinemas. The zinc lining of the boxes had to be soldered down and the film caught light from the workman's soldering tool. Tragically, the man lost his life and Pyke was prosecuted for negligence. The heat from the blaze was so intense that it forced up paving stones above the basement ceiling.

The main effect of the Act was to ensure that the source of film projection be situated outside the body of the auditorium; that there was a solid wall between the seating area and the projection room; and that the entrance to the projection room was from the open air and not through the foyer. The portholes between projection room and hall had to be glazed and fitted with fireproof shutters that could be lowered quickly to further reduce the risk of fire spreading. The other main requirement was for adequate audience escape routes and the provision of at least rudimentary fire-fighting equipment such as damp blankets and buckets of dry sand. In addition, some local authorities, such as the old London County Council, had their own safety and licensing requirements which, later on when audiences increased in size, became more draconian; normal exit doors had to open outwards, and emergency exits had to be fitted with 'panic' bolts, thus the ubiquitous phrase 'Push Bar To Open' was born. Building regulations for projection rooms became more stringent, so that the film rewind room had to be separated from the actual operating box by a solid wall with a fire-resistant self-closing door. Access to the projection room sometimes became a tortuous route across wet and windy roofs, verging on the terrifying. One of the worst examples was the approach the unfortunate

Electric, Portobello Road, west London, 1910

projectionist of the Rex cinema, Berkhamsted, had to take. An innocuous looking door in the balcony foyer led onto a somewhat unsteady iron stair, swinging up in two directions and clinging to the exterior wall of the auditorium, this traverse finally ending in a projection room which appears almost as an afterthought by its architect.

As a result of the Act, many of the earlier shop conversions and other premises had to close, as they could not comply with the new regulations – how could a totally enclosed room suddenly accommodate an isolated projection suite? But such was the buoyancy of the film trade that the early entrepreneurs invested heavily in rebuilding or, more often, constructed a new building on a new site. We come therefore to the first great era of purpose-built buildings for the movies.

It is interesting to analyse the plans for these early cinemas to see how their architects dealt with the problem of where to place the projection room. Quite a number of designers reversed the orientation of the building so that the audience entered either side of the screen with the projection room at the far end of the hall. Thus the projection room was isolated safely from the public entrance and exit, and being at ground level, construction costs were kept to a minimum. The disadvantage to this plan was the unpleasant distraction for the audience of constantly opening and closing entrance doors. In general, this idea was not popular and projection rooms were soon settled into a position above the entrance foyer.

Between 1910 and the outbreak of the First World War in 1914, some 3500 cinemas are said to have established themselves; dozens, if not hundreds in 1910 alone. The quality of the pictures had also improved by this time, the disconcerting flicker having been largely eradicated. By 1913 there were 497 buildings showing films listed in London and its suburbs, while Birmingham had 40, Manchester 90, Edinburgh 44, and Glasgow 40. Liverpool, curiously, had very few, with only 22. Meanwhile, cinemas were also taking root in every other city and town in the country. So great was the volume of construction that a considerable number of this first generation of purpose-built cinemas have come down to us, even though few are actually still showing films. It is impossible to list all of them here and I only intend to mention some of the more notable examples, including those still in operation as cinemas.

Two particularly good examples are the Electric, Portobello Road in London and the Electric Palace, Harwich, similar in scale and architectural form, which are dealt with in detail on page 24.

Another fine, early purpose-built cinema, which has recently been listed, is the Duke of Yorks, Preston Circus, Brighton. Externally it is a more ambitious building than either the Electric

Palace at Harwich or the Electric, Portobello Road, although less of the original interior decoration survives. The Duke of Yorks opened on 22 September 1910, and was designed by C.E. Clayton for Violet Melnotte-Wyatt, an actress and early film exhibitor. The façade was originally crowned with twin domes. There were three windows at first-floor level, lighting an upper foyer. Much of the auditorium now dates from 1937, when the present balcony was installed, the Edwardian plaster decoration was removed and a new, wider proscenium was introduced. The Duke of Yorks has had a recent refurbishment and is still showing films. It therefore stands as one of the oldest operating cinemas in Britain.

Violet Melnotte-Wyatt is also reported to have been involved in the building of the Brixton Cinematograph Theatre in 1911, which became part of the Montagu Pyke circuit. Only the façade of this cinema still exists and the Edwardian decoration was reduced when it lost its luscious plaster swags from around the front windows. This may well have been an attempt at modernisation in the face of stiff competition in Brixton.

Montagu Alexander Pyke was a larger than life character and London's first circuit operator. He apparently conceived the idea of running cinemas while witnessing one of Hale's Tours in Oxford Street in London, around 1906. His first cinema, in Edgware Road, did not open until early 1909, but he went on to erect cinemas at an astonishing rate; two more in 1909, eight in 1910 and five more in the following year. Of these, only four exist in any recognisable

24

Electric Palace, Harwich, Essex, 1911

Electric, Portobello Road, London 1910
Architect: Gerald Seymour Valentin

Electric Palace, Harwich 1911
Architect: Harold Hooper

These two cinemas are complete and precious survivors from the earliest days of the purpose-built cinema.

The Electric opened as the Electric Cinema Theatre on 24 February 1910, which indicates that it must have been planned before the Cinematograph Act of 1909 became operative on the first day of 1910. The proprietors were prepared for the new safe era of the cinema, as the planning incorporated all the new regulations laid down by the Act. The architect, Gerald Seymour Valentin, provided a restrained frontage (but for a dome), which conceals a rectangular hall with an elliptical ceiling. There was space for an audience of some 600. Most remarkably, the almost square proscenium survives unscathed, together with the plaster panelling on the walls. Other features that have amazingly survived are the Edwardian paybox and terrazzo floor at the entrance.

The Electric Palace, Harwich, is a similar sized building dating from almost two years later, opening on 29 November 1911. Here the façade is more exuberant, as one would expect of a promoter who had originally been a travelling fairground showman before deciding to put down roots in the cinema business. The cinema took just eighteen weeks to build and it cost about £1500. The architect was Harold Hooper of Ipswich. As well as the grand entrance facing Kings Quay Street, there was a subsidiary door from the fish dock for the cheaper seats near the screen. The smelly fishermen 'down the front' would

have frequently to be sprayed by the usherettes. The Electric Palace was a real 'flea pit'.

Due to competition from a neighbouring larger and more modern cinema, and the early effects of television, the Electric Palace closed in 1956 to be forgotten until rediscovery in 1972 when it was amongst the first batch of cinemas to receive listed status. Subsequently, a building preservation trust lovingly restored the cinema, and today it provides film entertainment for the town. To date this is the only cinema in Britain to be so well treated.

The Electric Palace's London sister also found itself overtaken by competition, although somehow it stayed in business (with at one point the notorious murderer John Christie for a projectionist). It had a fruitful period with a young and enthusiastic following in the 1970s as the Electric Cinema Club, but has lost its way in recent years and is currently closed.

form – at Shepherd's Bush and Brixton, and at Great Windmill Street and Charing Cross Road in London's West End. The two latter cinemas showed their last films relatively recently, in 1990 and 1987 respectively. The Charing Cross Road cinema was the most elaborate Pyke was to build, with a double line of boxes, opera-house fashion, along the sides of the long auditorium – these provided poor viewing conditions for the film, but opera-house connotations were probably at the back of Pyke's mind and, most likely, that of his architect. Regrettably nothing remains of this sumptuous interior and the building now houses a nightclub. Pyke went bankrupt in 1914, disappeared from the film scene, and died in 1935, planning a come-back with a new chain of cinemas.

What is now the Ritzy cinema, Brixton, is another good example of a purpose-built Edwardian cinema. Until recently the auditorium remained largely in its original state, and only the façade had been altered. Built by Israel Davis, the Ritzy opened as the Electric Pavilion in March 1911, the architects being E.C. Homes and Lucas. No more prominent site for a cinema could have been found, in the centre of Brixton, opposite the dominating Lambeth Town Hall completed only three years before, and even more remarkable is that it has survived later development.

Several other Edwardian cinemas are still operating, where the flavour of the early purpose-built picture palace can still be glimpsed. What is now the Gate Cinema, Notting Hill Gate, has a long, narrow interior with a virtually level floor and no balcony, but fine plaster decoration to the walls and ceiling, although the original proscenium has long since been covered over and the street front rebuilt. The previously mentioned Empress Electric Theatre in Upper Street, Islington, designed by Boreham and Gladding, opened in October 1913. It started life as a shop conversion on the same site operated by the Pesaresi brothers, which was so successful that they bought adjoining properties and had them all demolished and rebuilt as the present building. The passing of time has wrought damage to the fabric, but the great arch over the entrance still welcomes patrons to the Screen on the Green, as it is now known, the most familiar of impresario Romaine Hart's small and carefully controlled chain. The recent neon adornments above the façade, while not being in any way authentic, do at least cheer up Islington Green at night and loudly announce 'entertainment' to passers-by.

Another antique London building still doing good service for the movies is, at the time of writing, still operating as the MGM Cannon in King's Road, Chelsea. According to Malcolm Webb's *Greater London's Suburban Cinemas*, it first appeared on the scene

as the Palaseum in 1910 (architect A.W. Hudson), with a seating capacity of 960, certainly a good size for its date. This building, however, has suffered even more than the Empress in Islington, as, being so large, it has been heavily subdivided internally into four tiny 'screens' on the first floor, and the valuable long frontage to the King's Road at ground level has had to take a row of shop units.

Out of London, a notable early purpose-built cinema still operating is the Scala, Ilkeston, Derbyshire of 1913, a good enough example to have been listed Grade II*. Many more cinema buildings still exist as bingo and snooker halls or nightclubs; others have passed out of entertainment usage of any kind. Architecturally outstanding among these survivors is the Tower, Anlaby Road, Hull, by J. Percival Binks, opened in 1914. It has a fascinating façade, basically French baroque in inspiration, with very Parisian domes, but behind the upper level portico an art-nouveau arch encloses a glazed screen with a distinctly oriental flavour. Of similar interest, and also listed, are the former Salford Cinema (later the Rex), Chapel Street, Salford of 1912 and the Gainsborough, Sudbury in Suffolk of the same year. The Picture Palace, Jeune Street, Oxford, of 1911, was designed by John R. Wilkins and erected by one Frank Stuart, landlord of the Elm Tree pub next-door. This only lasted until the early 1920s when it became a furniture store, to lie dormant until 1976 when it sprang back into life as the Penultimate Picture Palace. The foyer retains its original paybox and it was

Tower, Hull, East Yorkshire, 1914

Electric Pavilion (now the Ritzy),
Brixton, south London, 1911

mainly for this reason that it was listed. Following another period of closure, it has reopened as the Ultimate Picture Palace. An original paybox also survives at the former Grove Picture Palace, in Stratford, east London. Ignoring an ugly asbestos street canopy, the façade presents an appearance unchanged from its July 1910 opening date. By the Second World War strong competition from other cinemas in the centre of Stratford had killed the Grove and the building became a warehouse, with a mezzanine floor inserted to create additional storage space. Despite the fine front, the fact that the auditorium has been so damaged has disqualified the Grove for listing.

Moving up to Scotland, an important listed Edwardian cinema is the Salon, Vinicombe Street, Glasgow, of 1913, by Thomas Baird Junior. It is recorded as having excellent plasterwork and back-lit decorative stained glass. The Salon was operating until 1992, but a rationalisation scheme by the exhibitor to confine their activities to their nearby Grosvenor cinema resulted in closure, although a

vigorous campaign has tried to reverse the situation.

So many of these early picture palaces have been lost altogether; space prevents itemising them all, but two in London must be mentioned. First, the Walpole Picture Theatre, Bond Street, Ealing, where in 1912 the architect John Stanley Beard applied a splendid new faience front to a 1908 former roller skating rink. The Walpole was demolished in 1981, but the faience front was saved, and repositioned at the rear of the replacement building, although it became somewhat damaged in the process. Beard, a great exponent of the use of faience, went on to design some excellent, if stylistically slightly eccentric schemes in subsequent decades. Second, the Palace, Kentish Town of 1913, designed by the same architect. The Palace survived until 1959, after which it was converted into offices. Luckily, the cinema was recorded in its Edwardian heyday by one of the foremost photographers of architecture and interiors of those times, Harry Bedford Lemere, in whose images the elegant interior is revealed.

Palace, Kentish Town, north London, 1913

Palace, Kentish Town, north London, 1913

5: The Edwardian Luxury Cinema

In the cinemas dealt with in the previous chapter, the planning and architectural form were relatively uncomplicated. The buildings consisted of a simple rectangular hall onto which was applied an elaborately decorated façade to attract the public. Sometimes a balcony would be added to gain extra seating capacity. Where a balcony was included, it would usually be flat fronted, although the more sophisticated examples, such as the Palace, Kentish Town, might have a balcony with a curved front, in emulation of contemporary live theatres. In the more ambitious projects, the balcony would be cantilevered rather than relying on loadbearing columns; the cantilevered balcony, developed at the end of the nineteenth century, had been used to most dramatic effect by the music hall architect Frank Matcham in the design of his theatres built during the variety boom years of 1896 to 1910. Decoratively, cinemas followed the prevailing fashion for the baroque, a style much employed on public and commercial buildings at the time, but which evolved into neo-classicism by the middle years of the century's second decade. Façades were often tiled in ceramic faience, a popular material with promoters and architects alike, who wished to imbue their cinemas with an image of pristine modernity, be-

lieving that its smooth surface would repel grime present in the heavily polluted atmosphere of cities at the time.

Cinemas of greater complexity soon started to appear; sometimes they were part of developments incorporating offices, flats or shops. They began to acquire extensive and elaborately decorated waiting areas and restaurant facilities, and to ape and even surpass the decorative luxury of the theatre. Architecturally, the special form of the cinema started to evolve away from the rectangular hall. Architects, realising that the best viewing location for film was neither in the front row of the stalls nor in a remote seat at the top of the balcony, experimented with the architectural form of the auditorium, introducing a splay to the proscenium flank walls, such as at the Palladium, Brixton, or a curved splay, such as at the Regent, Chelmsford, even creating an ellipse in the plan of the West End cinema in Coventry Street, London.

The Picture House, New Street, Birmingham, which opened in October 1910, was an early example of this new, more complex type of cinema building. The auditorium, seating 650, was still basically a rectangular hall, but of significance was the means of entry, through the ground floor of a four-storey commercial office building; the cinema had matured to become part of the big city scene. The Picture House was a promotion of Provincial Cinematograph Theatres, a company established in November 1909, with the purpose of creating the first nationwide cinema circuit. The foundation of this concern indicates how serious was the belief in the commercial potential of cinema construction. This company was by far the most highly capitalised of cinema operators to date. The scheme, designed by Nicol and Nicol of Birmingham, and Naylor and Sale of Derby, included a generous foyer, waiting areas and a lounge in the fashionable and elegant Adam style. An eight-piece orchestra was provided, along with a curious Edwardian musical instrument named the 'Animatophone', to accompany the films. This palace of the pictures proved too popular for its own good and had only a short life, closing in 1926, by which time PCT had opened a larger cinema nearby, adapted from a most unsuitable Victorian hall. The Picture House was converted into a shopping arcade, but the building itself survived the reconstruction of central Birmingham during the 1960s.

Similar lavish PCT 'Picture Houses' were constructed during 1910 in Glasgow, Leicester, Dublin, Manchester and Edinburgh. So successful were they that in the last three cities second PCT cinemas were opened. Particularly lavish was their New Picture House of 1913 created out of the banqueting hall of the Royal Hotel in Princes Street, Edinburgh. By 1913 the fashion for flamboyant baroque was on the wane and the architects, Robert Atkinson and George Alexander, provided an essay in neo-classical severity suitable for the 'Athens of the North', prescribing a coffered ceiling in the long narrow auditorium, Roman cross-framing in the balcony fronts and a marble-lined foyer. In contrast, however, one of the two tearooms was panelled with Louis XVI marquetry, redolent of the luxurious Pullman trains of the era. A highlight in the history of the New Picture House was the newsreel of the 1922 Derby, parachuted from a bi-plane which had flown directly from Epsom racecourse to enable the film to be screened in Edinburgh on the same day. Later, Princes Street became the domain of retail premises and the cinema closed in 1951 to make way for a department store with a new hotel above.

The Futurist in John Bright Street, Birmingham was a similarly lavish cinema, dating from the First World War years. Here the developer was Solomon Levy who, on a less ambitious scale than PCT, established a circuit of cinemas in provincial cities. The Futurist project, in which others besides Levy were involved, germinated in 1915, but the difficulties of retaining labour and finding building supplies in the First World War prevented opening until July 1919. Levy's architects for both the Scala and the Futurist were Essex and Goodman. For the Futurist, they designed a bold front in Flemish Renaissance style, executed in Midlands red brick with buff terracotta dressings. The foyer has a sturdy staircase with a balustrade constructed of the same terracotta, while the auditorium was enlivened with strange whimsical wall paintings of film 'vamps' and woodland scenes by Val Prince and Erskine Williams, reminiscent of contemporary film posters. The proscenium was heavily draped in Regency-style curtains. The Futurist is recorded as being the first cinema (at least in the Midlands) to have screen curtains or 'tabs' — in photographs of early cinemas they are absent. The interior of the Futurist was subdivided in 1981 and closed in 1993, but whatever happens to this unlisted cinema, it is to be hoped that the pleasing main front will be preserved.

It is worth examining in detail the three cinemas with innovatory planning mentioned earlier. First, the West End Cinema Theatre of 1913, with an elliptical auditorium ingeniously fitted into a compact site at the rear of pre-existing nineteenth-century buildings. The beaux arts-inspired plan was by an architect of French origin, Hippolyte Blanc, while the sumptuous French rococo interior was the inspiration of a designer with a most English sounding name, Horace Gilbert. While not being the largest, it was certainly the most opulent of London's pre-First World War cinemas, the intention being to compete with the belle-époque luxury of the latest Shaftesbury Avenue playhouses, and to attract the 'carriage trade'. Entrance to the cinema was through an elegant Louis XVI foyer and the walls of the auditorium were adorned with pavilion 'loges', terminating the ends of the balcony. A restaurant occupied the basement, and this feature would be incorporated in at least two other central London cinema developments of the time. The West End's elliptical layout broke with the 'long hall' type of plan, creating an atmosphere of greater intimacy and dispensing with the poor-visibility seating furthest from the screen.

The pavilion boxes appear again in the second example, the Palladium, Brixton, also of 1913, designed by Gilbert Booth. Thirdly, in the Regent, Chelmsford, which opened in 1916, the architect Francis Burdett Ward did not produce an elliptical plan but focused the auditorium walls onto the proscenium in a splay formation. It too has pavilion boxes terminating the balcony front. The Regent had a deep stage, which must make it among the first purpose-built cinemas to be equipped for stage entertainment as well as film. The West End cinema, however, was intended purely for showing movies, with no stage of any description behind the screen. Being slightly later, the interior decoration of the Regent was less florid than in the West End or the Palladium. The West End Cinema Theatre, later named the Rialto, has been closed since

Palladium, Brixton, south London, 1913

West End Cinema Theatre (renamed the Rialto in 1924), Coventry Street, London, 1913

1982. Gilbert Booth's Palladium, Brixton, had an attractive stone front continuing the cornice of the adjacent and almost contemporary Lambeth Town Hall. The cinema façade became obscured by cement render in later years and, tragically, the auditorium was damaged in a fire during the early 1980s. The Regent, Chelmsford, after being carefully maintained by that most concerned and responsible of exhibitors, Shipman and King, is now preserved by bingo until such time as some more creative use can be found for this fine building.

The general form of the Ionic, Golders Green, was still that of a long rectangular hall, but the architect, 'Major' W. J. King, transformed it with a sinuous balcony front which looped its way around the auditorium, dictating the configuration of the seats, from some of which there could only have been a squinting glimpse of the screen. Behind them a parade of private boxes lined the walls. Two of the boxes, flanking the proscenium, were purely intended for decorative effect as they actually faced away from the screen into the body of the hall. This was a cinema in opera-house attire; impractical as a 'machine for watching the movies' it may have been, but the Ionic had great charm, with the atmosphere of a court theatre, like the preserve of some Ruritanian potentate. The great ballerina Anna Pavlova performed the opening ceremony in

1913. A supermarket marks the site today with a more serviceable replacement cinema in the basement.

Further pre-First World War London cinemas of exceptional decorative interest included the rococo style Pavilion, Hackney (1914), designed by George Billings, which featured similar gazebo boxes to provide interest in the long flank walls (demolished 1972); the Angel Picture Theatre, of 1913, by H. Courtnay Constantine (one of the first architects to emerge as a cinema specialist), which had a barrel-shaped ceiling in the auditorium, and arcades in the flanking walls behind which lay aisles, as in a church; and the Cinema House, in Oxford Street, with an oak-panelled interior in Jacobean country house style, the work of Melville Seth-Ward in 1910. All three auditoria are now but memories, although the one-hundred-foot high tower and a section of foyer from the Angel Picture Theatre survive and are listed. Out of London, the Villa Cross Picture House, Birmingham, displayed crisp Edwardian detailing of notable quality, in which plaster scrolls extolled the virtue of film in such ringing phrases as 'The World Before Your Eyes'. The Regent in the then enormously popular resort of Great Yarmouth, was one of the most ambitious cinemas yet built. The Regent, like its sister in Chelmsford, was the creation of the architect Francis Burdett Ward, and was built for the prominent East

Grange, Kilburn, north London, 1914

Ionic, Golders Green, north London, 1913

Anglian exhibitor, Frederick Holmes Cooper. The cinema seated over 1600 holidaymakers in Edwardian luxury. The interior style was advertised as Louis XIV, and executed in tones of dove grey, rose and pompadour and antique gold. An unusual feature was the steep rake of the main floor which improved viewing of the screen above many a feathered chapeau. Upstairs, tea-time delicacies were dispensed in a panelled restaurant furnished with high-backed chairs and starched tablecloths, like the stuffy middle-class dining rooms of the era, while beguiling putti scampered amidst a plaster landscape of cornucopia and bulbous swags in the surrounding frieze. Much of this grandeur survives today to the sound of the bingo caller's intonations.

Less sumptuous but of even greater scale was the Grange cinema in the north-west London suburb of Kilburn, named after the small park which lies behind the building. It opened at the end of July 1914, with a film version of *She Stoops to Conquer*. The Grange was the culmination of the first age of cinema construction prior to the First World War, its 2028 seats making it not only the largest cinema in London, but probably also in Britain at that time. The densely populated district of Kilburn proved ripe territory for monster cinemas, as history repeated itself in the second great age of construction between the two wars, when the Gaumont State cinema, sited almost opposite the Grange and seating over 4000, opened in 1937. The Grange, an early work by Edward Stone, an architect who came to prominence in cinema design during the late 1920s, can still be seen. The body of the cinema lies parallel to Kilburn High Road behind a row of integral shops, above which stands a spacious apartment, originally the tearoom, which one entered from a grand double-height foyer on the corner. In addition to the main balcony, the auditorium has side galleries, or 'slips', extending towards the proscenium, in the manner of a traditional opera house. In this respect there is a planning analogy with the Ionic, although there the overall effect was more exciting due to the continuous line of snaking balconies. The Grange ceased to show films in 1975, subsequently becoming a dance hall. A work by another architect who was to gain respect as a versatile cinema designer during the late 1920s, George Coles, was the Kingsland Empire, Dalston, north-east London, of 1915. Built on the site of an earlier cinema, it had a dome above the corner façade, and a high auditorium with a large balcony. The building was reconstructed by Frederick Bromige in 1937, and is now the Rio cinema.

For the Edwardian cinema a showy façade to attract the crowds was essential. It continued the tradition set by the fairground bioscope where a gaudy front disguised the makeshift construction which lay behind. A fine example already mentioned existed in the

form of the Palace, Kentish Town, London, which proudly displayed its date of opening, 1913, in a cartouche above the entrance. Most remarkable was the Carlton, Swansea, built a year later. Although this cinema has long since been closed, the towering frontage, designed by the grandiloquently named Sir Charles Tamlin Ruthen, still looms over Welsh shoppers. In this unique composition, an extraordinary three-storey glazed bay bursts forth as a centrepiece of a baroque assemblage, curving in at the top as a semi-dome. The Corona, Gorton, Manchester, of 1912, had a façade in green and white faience with twin towers like a medieval cathedral, while two other cinemas, the Kings Hall, Lewisham (1912), in south-east London, and the Cinema House in Rotherham (1914), dallied with the Moorish style, a portent of the exotic cinema fronts of the late 1920s. The search for a style to express the new medium had begun.

Corona, Gorton, Manchester, 1912

6: The Early 1920s: The First 'Super Cinemas'

The Great War period, 1914-18, was an era of huge film popularity, when Charlie Chaplin entertained the world and early Hollywood productions really took a grip of our screens. English film production was making strides from studios at Islington and Walton-on-Thames, but British efforts were primarily directed towards the events in Flanders and Northern France, so allowing American film distributors a clear field. Restrictions on construction were imposed, and although cinemas were opening during the war, they were schemes that had started before the outbreak of hostilities, such as the Futurist, Birmingham, already mentioned.

In 1914, the trade paper, the *Kinematograph and Lantern Weekly* (the 'lantern' part of the title was soon dropped) launched the *Kinematograph Year Book* as a guide for those in the industry. Besides lists of film titles available, extracts from the various cinema regulation acts, suppliers and a 'who's who' section, this useful publication also listed every regularly operating commercial cinema during each of the subsequent fifty-seven years, until it ceased publication in 1970. The 1921 edition estimated that there were already some 4000 cinemas in Britain, not far short of the maximum number ever to operate in Britain, 4800 in 1949. However, in 1921,

the average seating capacity was around 600, much smaller than the 2000- and 3000-seater cinemas built during the heyday of the late 1920s and throughout the 1930s.

By 1921 the 'block booking' system had been introduced from America; by making a greater number of prints available, films could be shown more widely and therefore benefit from increased advertising by the distributor. It was at this time that the pattern of film distribution was laid down, remaining unchanged until the 1970s, by which time the number of outlets had been drastically reduced. Wherever you lived, you could calculate how long it would be before a particular film reached your local cinema. Because of the greater demand caused by block booking, the 1921 *Kinematograph Year Book* suggested that another 2000 cinemas could be filled, but in practice, many of the older halls gradually disappeared to be replaced by larger cinemas.

It was around 1920 that many live theatres were forced to turn to movies, such was the demand for film entertainment. A continuing reminder of this time is the Coronet, Notting Hill Gate in west London. Designed by W.G.R. Sprague and dating from 1898, it was never particularly successful as a theatre and showed its first films

Stoll Picture Theatre, Kingsway,
London, in use as a cinema from 1917

in 1916. It converted full time to movies in 1923, and although its gallery has been disused for many years, the Coronet has not been seriously altered. To a true lover of the theatre, of course, such a building is wasted as the stage stands deserted behind an echoing cinema screen. Another example of theatre turning to film is the Grand, Clapham Junction, in south London (designed by E.A. Woodrow, 1900), where the rare Chinese-style auditorium has survived intact through periods of films and bingo to become a music venue. The Theatre Royal in Peter Street, Manchester, with a distinguished early Victorian façade, was internally reconstructed as a full-time cinema in 1921, removing a stage fifty-feet deep in the process. This listed theatre still survives, although it is now used for other purposes. These theatre conversions were early casualties during the late 1950s and early 1960s, when cinemas were closing down with great rapidity. They were regarded as draughty old barns with dreadful sight-lines, and many became temporary television studios before the wrecker's ball made short work of their faded interiors.

The entertainment centre of cities constantly changes as commerce takes over. One of the most notorious of theatres built in the wrong place was the imperiously named London Opera House, which opened in 1911 on Kingsway, then London's new Parisian boulevard. The theatre was a venture to break the monopoly on grand opera controlled by the Covent Garden Opera House, but it failed to attract the great singing stars, so vital at the time, and reopened as Oswald Stoll's eponymous Picture Theatre in 1917. It was successful throughout the 1920s, but the out-of-the-way location and the greater competition from cinemas in Leicester Square started to reduce audiences. The Stoll lingered on until 1940, when poor attendance at the height of the war-time blitz forced it to close. One of the great London theatre losses, the Stoll was demolished in 1957 to make way for an office block with a smaller auditorium in the basement.

Building restrictions were lifted from 1919, and in 1920 there was a flurry of openings, with grander, more confident buildings, and a balcony becoming almost standard. One of the most notable examples of this new style of building was the Dalston Picture Theatre in Hackney, north-east London, designed by Frederick Edward Jones and Robert Cromie. It was built by E.E. Lyons and Thomas Underwood to be part of their Biocolor Picture Theatre circuit. The *Kinematograph Weekly* described the Dalston Picture Theatre as a 'super cinema', possibly one of the first occasions when this epithet was used. It was a reconstruction of the failed Dalston Circus of 1866, which had been in use as a variety theatre. The trade journal describes the auditorium decoration as 'freely treated Greek' in cream and gold, indicating that the colour scheme was still in Edwardian vein. Around the balcony walls electric lamps simulating flaming torchères were mounted on brass pedestals; the most expensive front circle seats were said to be upholstered in gold silk, and the carpets were black with a gold pattern. The whole effect was termed 'distinctly rich without being objectionably gaudy'. There was a narrow stage with an aluminium screen painted directly on the plaster wall, surrounded by purple and silver drapery onto which subdued lights played during the film. In the pit there was an orchestra of twenty-six musicians while the café also had a ladies' quartet. In order to gain a level projection throw, the operating box was placed at the rear of the stalls. The seating capacity was stated to be nearly 3000, undoubtedly an exaggeration. The Biocolor circuit became a constituent part of the Gaumont-British Picture Corporation when this company was formed in 1927. Renamed Gaumont in 1951, the Dalston Picture Theatre closed nine years later and became a car auction hall with a nightclub in what was the foyer. The fibrous plaster decoration was eventually torn off the lower parts of the walls to reveal bare brickwork at stalls level, like a gigantic stage set suspended from the flies.

The Dalston Picture Theatre was quite one of the grandest cinemas at the time, but one of the strangest to be built that year was the King's Cross Cinema situated near the London station of the same name. It was designed by H. Courtenay Constantine and externally it appears a solid classical structure placed on a corner, which Constantine uses to effect with a rotunda and dome. Little would one believe that it is hoisted above a four-track railway divided between the London Underground and a cross-town link, at that time still the preserve of raucous steam trains. This extraordinary site used the 'air rights' over the railway, although the location, at the hub of a great transport interchange point, was, at that time, excellent. A further example from that year is the former Beau Nash Picture House in Bath, now listed and still, amazingly, operating as a cinema under the ABC banner. It is an instance of rapid reconstruction on the site of an existing cinema which had only opened in 1910, indicating that business was so profitable that further expansion was necessary just ten years later. The architect was a local man, Alfred J. Taylor, and the street front remains almost unaltered, full of charming period appeal, there being no proper foyer, with the stairs to the balcony rising almost directly from the pavement.

In 1921-2, a number of cinemas of significance opened in the heart of four major British cities. The Elite Picture Theatre, Nottingham, designed by Adamson and Kinns, opened in August 1921. In this central location it was worth acquiring more land than was strictly necessary for the cinema, which left sufficient room for a substantial four-storey block of offices to be incorporated in the development. For this reason it is of interest, being an early example of a cinema forming part of a comprehensive redevelopment, which also incorporated a sequence of restaurants and Masonic lodges, each decorated in a different historical style.

The Capitol, Cardiff, opened on Boxing Day in the same year. It was a much larger building with over 2800 seats, and probably took the laurels from the Grange, Kilburn for being the largest purpose-built cinema in Britain at the time. It had an extremely broad but shallow, auditorium and local legend has it that it was originally intended to be constructed the other way round, i.e. long and narrow. The Capitol was the only cinema designed by the architect R.S. Phillips. It became a fashionable local venue and in the 1930s the showcase for Paramount films in Wales. Such a large cinema was unlikely to survive in a prime city-centre position and, indeed, it has now disappeared.

The third example, which had a life of less than twenty years — a victim of overseating or 'redundancy', as it was known in the trade — was the most impressive of this group. The Piccadilly cinema of 1922 faced the gardens of the same name in Manchester. The elegant façade (in Doulton 'Carraraware') can still be seen, but the interior was lost when the building became a clothing store before the Second World War, when the focus of entertainment in central Manchester moved half a mile west to Oxford Street. Twin

sets of doors, presumably to segregate the entrance from the exit, were separated by shop units. A modest 'crush hall', or foyer, led to a square but asymmetrical auditorium — the plans indicate a block of seats to one side which only indirectly faced the screen and must have had poor sight-lines. Above were two cantilevered balconies, which accounted for the bulk of the 2324 seats, and there were lifts to reach them. The second balcony was an extraordinary asymmetrical shape, which must have been visually disconcerting. Neither the variety theatre architect Frank Matcham, nor the specialist cinema architects after him, however, would have found this permissible, symmetry being all important to these perfectionists of planning. The contemporary report in the *Builder* magazine makes special mention of the ventilating system which changed the air every ten minutes. No reference is made to a refrigeration plant, therefore it could not be termed an air-conditioning system in the modern sense. Refreshments were provided by a huge restaurant seating 500 people, occupying almost the entire basement area, and a café on the mezzanine floor of the crush hall. Decoratively, the architect Percy Hothersall employed the fashionable neoclassical style with a splendid Greek frieze high above the arched proscenium. The Piccadilly justified the accolade 'movie palace', deserved of such an ambitious complex, and it would now be better known were it not for its early demise.

Last of this group was the Majestic, situated opposite the main station at Leeds. It was designed by Pascal J. Steinlet and opened

Dalston Picture Theatre, north-east London, 1920

in 1922. Steinlet studied at the Beaux Arts School in Paris, a training made obvious by his suave and curvaceous frontage for the cinema. The exterior was clad in 'Marmo', an imitation marble supplied by the Leeds Fireclay Company. Stylistically, there is a similarity between the Majestic and the Piccadilly in that they both had French-inspired exteriors, while internally they played with the Neo-Greek, in vogue at the time but perhaps more suited to swimming pools or municipal offices than entertainment venues. Steinlet's plan cleverly uses the maximum space available, although the complex layout might have been confusing for the public, there being entrances in both flanking streets and on the corner facing the City Square. This corner entrance only led to stairs down to a basement restaurant and ballroom. Behind these stairs was the screen, and the auditorium fanned out beyond. No doubt this plan was suggested by the exigencies of a difficult site, but it is an early example of the fan-shaped cinema plan, advocated by the architect Robert Atkinson. A false ceiling in the auditorium, installed in 1969, obscured much of the frieze above the proscenium and the large coffered saucer dome. The Majestic closed as a bingo hall in 1995, but hopefully its future is ensured, as it has listed status.

These cinemas were expensive schemes in high-profile locations. We will now look at examples of more typical projects of the period, which survive. The first is the Coronation, Manor Park, in east London, of 1921. The name commemorates the coronation of George V in 1910, the date when the previous cinema opened on the site – another example of the disposable cinema, totally reconstructed after only ten years' service. The new Coronation was designed by Clifford Aish and consisted of a large rectangular auditorium arranged parallel with the street frontage. The audience capacity was high, with some 1845 seats. The architectural form is that of a long low hall. Many architects had not learnt how to cope with the 'tunnel effect' in auditorium design and the lack of intimacy inherent in this type of building. We shall see later on how Aish and other architects managed to disguise the problem and produce more satisfactory interiors. The Coronation stands today and retains good plasterwork, albeit still rather Edwardian in flavour, above and behind a false ceiling installed for the present snooker use.

The Art cinema in Bury, Lancashire, of 1922, has an auditorium quite theatrical in feeling, with stage boxes. The entrance is in the centre of a long façade and access to the stalls is directly behind it, half-way down the auditorium. The scheme is more typical of theatre planning than cinema, where entrance doors need to be inconspicuously placed for continuous film performance. The architect was Albert Winstanley, who had adapted the original Art Picture House out of a baptist chapel on the site. The Art is now a well maintained bingo hall and is listed.

The front of the Picture House, Chesterfield, of 1923, was clad in fake timber framing to accord with the town's sense of history – other contemporary buildings here were also being tricked out in the same fancy dress. Internally, however, things were slavishly classical with a frieze of plaster fauns and maidens frolicking over the stage, and eagles with outstretched wings soaring around the auditorium. The Picture House had a large ballroom as well as a café. The complex survives today as the Winding Wheel (a name appropriate for a district steeped in coal mining history), a multi-purpose entertainment venue.

In these same years, two cinemas of national significance appeared in London and Brighton. The Regent, Brighton of 1921 broke new ground in the construction of the large 'super cinema'. The Regent is very much the precursor of the 'movie palace style' in Britain. It was designed by Robert Atkinson, an architect who included cinemas in a range of commissions from an art gallery (the Barber Institute in Birmingham) to newspaper offices (the Jazz Moderne entrance hall of the Daily Express building in Fleet Street, London). The Regent was the brainchild of F.E. Adams, managing director of Provincial Cinematograph Theatres, a company always in the vanguard of cinema developments right up to its amalgamation with Gaumont-British in 1928. The name 'Regent', although used elsewhere, was particularly appropriate for Brighton, with its historical connections with the Prince Regent. For a full description of the Regent, turn to page 42.

The Pavilion, Shepherd's Bush, in west London, opened in August 1923. It was designed by Frank Verity and is an instance of an exhibitor employing a leading non-specialist architect with a fashionable practice; Verity had, after all, been called in by Edward VII after his accession to the throne in 1901, to recast Queen Victoria's ballroom at Buckingham Palace in the latest spirit of the 'entente cordiale'. Verity was a master of luxury blocks of flats in smart districts of central London, but he also had a background in designing theatres through his partnership with his father, Thomas Verity. However, Frank Verity had never designed anything remotely like the Pavilion before (and neither had any other architect), its external appearance being quite different from other theatre or cinema buildings. The Pavilion continued the Edwardian preoccupation with monumentality and it has this in common with the great edifices of stone and concrete being erected at the time by such architects as Sir Edwin Cooper. To the left of the great façade is an immensely solid, superbly proportioned, entrance block with a two-storey arched window flanked by smaller apertures, topped by

Piccadilly, Manchester, 1922

Majestic, Leeds, West Yorkshire, 1922

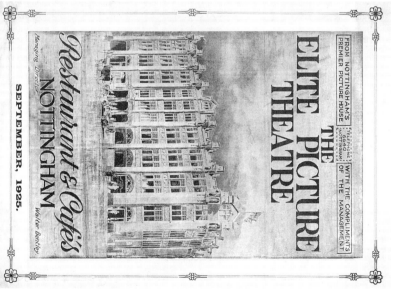

Programme for the Elite Picture Theatre, Nottingham, 1921

Pavilion, Shepherd's Bush,
west London, 1923

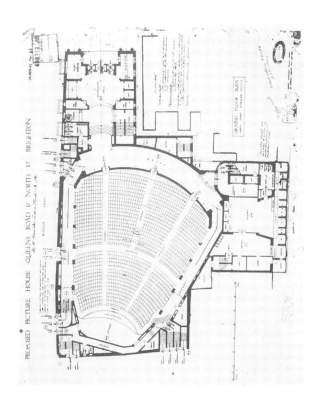

Robert Atkinson's revolutionary fan-shaped plan
for the Regent, Brighton, East Sussex, 1921

segmental pediments. The auditorium block, built parallel to the street, is set back with a lower range in front. This arrangement seems to accentuate the colossal scale. In the upper half of the auditorium, which would otherwise be blank brickwork, are three gigantic blind lunette windows. Internally, Verity designed in the full glory of the Roman Empire – coffering, tripod funerary urns, stencil decoration and even fake drapery. For the Pavilion, Verity was awarded the Royal Institute of British Architects' bronze medal in 1924 for the best London street frontage. The jury, which included Sir Edwin Lutyens, found the building 'an imposing structure of brick and stone in which the former material, especially, is used with great imagination'. Externally, Verity's inspiration is from the great baths of antiquity – Diocletian via the beaux arts. Within only a very short time the taste for the monumental could find renewed expression through the fashion for things Egyptian fostered by the discovery of Tutankhamun's treasure in 1922. At any rate, Verity and the Pavilion achieved something at the time to help cinema architecture to be taken seriously. Although he designed many other interesting cinemas, Verity never again produced anything so radical.

The Pavilion was the greatest project of the Israel Davis circuit to date. Davis had built up a small circuit from before the Great War and there was concern in the cinema exhibition trade as to whether such a vast cinema (it held 2767 people) could be regularly filled in a location then regarded as suburbia. The western side of Shepherd's Bush Green had twice before been selected for entertainment buildings (the Empire theatre of 1903, and an early Montagu Pyke cinema in 1910) and therefore Davis must have felt confident of the location with its high density of population, and multiplicity of public transport bringing audiences in from outlying areas. The pessimists were proved wrong, as the cinema was an instant success. Regrettably, the auditorium of the Pavilion was destroyed by bombing in the Second World War, and subsequently rebuilt in a different form. The exterior is ostensibly unchanged and the building is now listed.

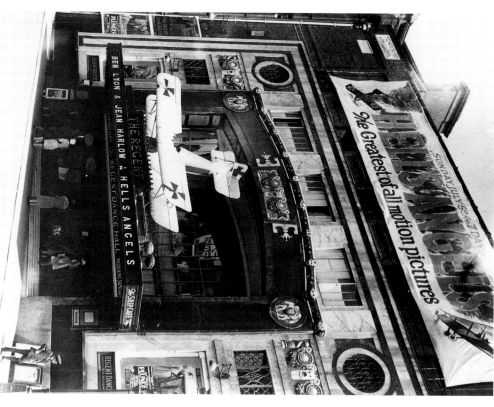

The Regent, Brighton 1921
Architect: Robert Atkinson

The promoters of the Regent – Provincial Cinematograph Theatres – acquired the site of this cinema in 1914, but work could not proceed immediately due to building restrictions during the First World War. During the war years film production techniques improved and attendances increased to the point where cinemas were unable to meet the demand. As a result, when peace came ambitious plans were drawn up for new and larger cinemas.

In 1919, an architect to the PCT company, Robert Atkinson, was commissioned by the Royal Institute of British Architects to visit the USA and write a report on American architectural education. With the Brighton project in mind, he took the opportunity while in the United States to study the latest developments in cinema design. It is likely that Atkinson visited Thomas Lamb's Capitol, New York, and its influence on the Regent is evident. The wide fan-shaped plan and superimposed proscenium arch of the Capitol were reproduced by Atkinson in the Regent, despite its awkward and irregular site. The Regent brought the opulent style of the American 'movie palace' to Britain.

Atkinson's first proposals for the principal front on Queens Road indicate a five-storey brick building with a semi-circular window above the entrance. This was abandoned in favour of an increased use of faience, surrounding an arched proscenium-like opening above the entrance as a frame for two levels of glazing. This motif was later adapted for cinema façades elsewhere, for example, the Kensington, London (see Chapter 11). Inserted into the faience were colourful panels of classically derived motifs in 'Della Robbia ware' designed by Charles Doman.

The Regent, which seated 2200, opened without ceremony in July 1921. The predominant colours in the auditorium were warm shades of orange and vermilion, with figurative paintings for decoration. The elliptical proscenium arch was painted by Laurence Preston, principal of the Brighton School of Art, to represent a carnival procession. Painted scenes elsewhere were executed by Walter Bayes and Walpole Champneys.

Originally a ballroom had been planned for the basement, but the twenty-four hour production needed to construct it caused so much disruption to the neighbours that the scheme had to be abandoned in favour of a ballroom built on the roof, as a second phase in 1923, to replace an unrealised winter-garden. With two restaurants and a tearoom, the Regent was indeed a palace of varied pleasures.

The Regent was a popular cinema for fifty-one years until the then owners, Rank, decided to close their three cinemas in Brighton, transferring operations to an anonymous former ice rink on the sea-front. The last vestiges of the Regent disappeared in 1977, although some of Doman's decorative plaques survive in the Brighton museum and in private hands.

7: The American Movie Palace

While Britain had certainly produced some fine cinemas by 1925, the cinema buildings in America were larger and more elaborate, and there were many more of them. Even by 1915 there were an estimated 25,000 cinemas in the USA, with an average of 6,000,000 admissions daily. Even taking into account the population ratio of Britain to the United States, the pro rata number of cinemas was still greater in the USA than in the UK. This was no doubt due to the higher standard of living in the USA, but also to a greater movie awareness and to the fact that the distributors were marketing an indigenous product to which everyone could relate – a combination which could not fail to inspire a compulsive following. Neither had the Great War inhibited cinema building as it had done in Britain; cinemas continued to open in the States throughout this period.

In the early days, however, Britain and the USA were following very similar paths in terms of cinema development. Thousands of shop conversions were taking place, very quickly followed by substantial purpose-built cinemas such as the Dreamland theatre in Portland, Maine, of 1907. By 1914, the Strand on Broadway, New York, had been built, with 2958 seats, larger than any cinema in

Britain at the time. What is considered to be the first superior theatre built specifically for movies had opened in the previous year, in the form of the Regent in Harlem, New York, designed by the great cinema architect, Thomas Lamb. Lamb was born in Dundee, Scotland, in 1877 and came to the United States when he was twelve. He graduated in architecture at the Cooper Union in New York and was a building inspector for the city until 1909, when he was given his first architectural commission, the City cinema, for William Fox on 14th Street, then the centre of New York's movieland. Lamb designed some 300 cinemas and theatres altogether, not only in America but in other parts of the world, including the new Empire, Leicester Square in London. The Regent, New York, had a Venetian-style exterior and held 1845 New Yorkers in an interior of restrained classical style. Lamb went on to design many cinemas inspired by his compatriot Robert Adam.

This early phase of the movie palace culminated in another cinema by Lamb, the Capitol, on the corner of Broadway and 51st Street in New York. This building is reputed to have held in excess of 5000 spectators, and if this estimate is correct, then this scale of building was not to be exceeded for another eight years, when the elephantine Roxy on 7th Avenue came along. The nearest any British cinema had come to these proportions was Green's Playhouse in Glasgow, which had 4254 seats.

It was cinemas such as the Capitol which were visited by Robert Atkinson on his eleven-week fact-finding tour of the United States in 1919, prior to designing the Regent, Brighton, of 1921 (see page 42), in which one can detect obvious American parallels, particularly in its planning.

By the mid-1920s, American exhibitors were beginning to demand of their architects something other than French baroque and Robert Adam. In Chicago, Balaban and Katz had to implore their architects George and Cornelius Rapp to break with France for their new project in Randolph Street, which was to become the Oriental (1926). This they did somewhat reluctantly, but it is to their credit that they produced an entirely convincing essay in writing dragons' tails and elephants' tusks, with much looped-up drapery around the stage. Ben Hall, in his book *The Best Remaining Seats: The Story of the Golden Age of the Movie Palaces*, describes it as having 'hasheesh-dream decor'.

The architect C. Howard Crane came to prominence with three interiors for United Artists — in Los Angeles (1927), Chicago and Detroit (both of 1928), for which he thought up a frenzied Gothic style, with its origins in late medieval Spain and Portugal, but with a helping of Westminster's Henry VII chapel for good measure, although there was still room for murals depicting Mary Pickford, one of the founding 'United Artists'. Crane is best known for the two very similar 5000-seat cinemas he designed for William Fox in Detroit (1928) and St Louis (1929). Crane ultimately had a hand in the planning of the Radio City Music Hall in New York in 1932, and was responsible for cinemas in London; the Granada, Greenwich and the Gaumont, Holloway in 1937 and 1938 respectively.

New York was the scene, in March 1927, of the inauguration of the best known of American movie palaces, the Roxy, on the corner of 7th Avenue and 50th Street. This was to be the promoter Samuel Rothapfel's movie 'cathedral', where he could indulge his penchant for the largest and most ostentatious of everything. The seating capacity was staggering, at just eighty seats under 6000, only to be superseded in size by the Radio City Music Hall, which had 5960 seats. Rothapfel's architect was one Walter Ahlschlager, with decorative treatment by Harold Rambusch. Ben Hall relates Rothapfel's brief to Rambusch: 'Harold, I see my theater like the inside of a great bronze bowl – everything in tones of antique gold, warm, very, very rich, gorgeous.' The architectural style chosen was the Plateresque (the Spanish architectural form of the Renaissance, the term derived from the name for Spanish silversmiths, the

'plateros'). Everywhere were swirling Renaissance arabesque motifs, barley-sugar columns, heavy coffering and plagiarised pulpits from Iberia, and all undetailed surfaces were textured, distressed and burnished to achieve the desired effect. In a brilliant plan, the architect fitted an extreme example of a fan-shaped auditorium into a square site, with an adjacent cube accommodating an oval foyer, encircled by access stairs. Conceived as the ultimate cine-variety house, it boasted a huge stage, a rising orchestra platform and an organ which (while not being the largest of cinema organs) had to have three consoles, each on a separate elevator. The magic of the place was the total experience provided by the Roxy, one which was emulated wherever the super cinema palace was attempted. The name Roxy became a synonym for the luxury cinema, and many were spawned of the same name in Britain. A Gloria Swanson epic, *The Love of Sunya*, opened the Roxy, and she was also to provide its visual epitaph, as she posed in the summer of 1960 amid the shards of golden plaster of the wrecked foyer exposed to the unnatural daylight – a poignant image at the close of the movie palace era.

Roxy wanted his showplace to be spell-binding, to transport the audience away from their ordinary lives to a world of luxury and, ultimately, fantasy. The Great War was receding into memory, people were more affluent, and the spirit of the Roaring Twenties was alive; Roxy's request for a 'great bronze bowl' expressed the desire of his audiences for escape to the ideal life. The stars of the silent screen had to act with their eyes and be masters of mime; hypnotic shadows traversed engulfing cliff-like screens four storeys high, accompanied by the swelling music of transient romance – a fatal recipe for total slavery. To meet this insatiable appetite, cinema owners pressed their designers for innovation. Where could architects go after the 'bronze bowl', having explored France, Spain and permutations of the Italian Renaissance? Egyptian and Chinese were possible (the showman Sid Grauman's favourites in Hollywood Boulevard), but why not pretend that the film was being shown out of doors, dispense with the ceiling and imagine being in an evocative Mediterranean courtyard with fountains, ancient plastered walls, a statue or two, and a distant cypress tree, on a balmy summer night? The 'atmospheric' auditorium was born.

The 'atmospheric' interior was the invention of John Eberson, an Austrian electrical engineer, who emigrated to the United States in 1901 and settled in St Louis. He became involved in the installation of electrical equipment in theatres, turning to architecture in 1908, although he had no formal training. The practice seems to have been a success as he was awarded the appellation 'Opera House John', designing theatres and cinemas in traditional style across

Grauman's Egyptian, Hollywood, 1922

America's south and mid-west. However, he came up with something entirely new in the guise of the auditorium of the Majestic, Houston, Texas, in 1923. Here he developed his idea of the 'atmospheric' cinema, the decoration consisting of exterior architectural elements, such as a temple mounted high up to the right of the proscenium and pergolas further back above the balcony. And it was asymmetrical – features did not answer one another across the auditorium – but, most radical of all, was the fact that there appeared to be no ceiling. There *was* a ceiling, of course, but it was in the form of a giant featureless plaster dome stretching right across the auditorium from wall to wall, onto which were projected cloud effects, with tiny inset electric bulbs to represent the stars in the night sky. Eberson's initial training as an electrical engineer,

and by consequence, his predilection towards an architecture incorporating technically created illusion, was crucial to this development. There had been precursors elsewhere – 'semi-outdoor' schemes such as at the Cort theatre in Chicago, of 1909, by J.E. Pridmore and Thomas Lamb's Wintergarden theatre in Toronto, a double-decked theatre complex built in 1914, where the ceiling consists entirely of a leaf-clad pergola. The winter-garden, as a late nineteenth-century building type in Europe, often included a theatre or concert hall, where the indoor garden theme could cross-pollinate into auditorium design. The 'atmospheric' appealed to exhibitors, who not only appreciated the enhanced evocation of fantasy, but also the fact that 'atmospherics' were cheaper to build, possibly only a third of the cost of similar sized classical or 'hard

Capitol, New York, 1919

Majestic, Houston, Texas, 1923

top' interiors, as they became known. 'Atmospherics' (designed by other architects as well as Eberson) appeared all over the USA, varying the theme between Italian garden; Spanish street scene (the Tampa, in the city of the same name, Florida, 1928); Persian harem (Avalon, Chicago, 1927); Moorish fortress (Fox, Atlanta); Chinese (Pekin theatre in the eponymous town in Illinois, 1928); and, most eccentric of all, Dutch (Holland theatre, Bellfontaine, Ohio, 1931), complete with a windmill over the emergency exit door in the auditorium wall. Sometimes the foyer was also given the 'atmospheric' treatment, and the fantasy was known to extend to 'ladies' powder rooms' and 'gentlemen's retiring rooms', tricked out as the 'Harem's parlour' or the 'Caliph's den'.

Other fabulous interiors, such as in the two breathtaking Paradise cinemas, in Chicago (1928), and in the Bronx, New York (1929), were created by Eberson. In the former, a 'ride of the Valkyries' arose into the stratosphere above the proscenium, while the Bronx example was a Latin American wedding-cake cathedral incorporating copies of Italian statues, with electric doves wheeling into the distant cumulus. These two great picture palaces had a baby sister in Faribault, Minnesota, in which, beside the projection room switchboard, was a sign beseeching the operator 'not to turn on the clouds until the show starts' and to 'be sure the stars are turned off when leaving'.

This chapter has briefly covered the American influence on the movie palace in Britain, and we will see the development of 'atmospherics' in Britain in Chapter 13.

8: Hollywood
in the West End

The burgeoning Hollywood epic had to be experienced in a suitable setting. Not only was an auditorium of some dignity required, but these much publicised films could fill a substantial theatre for weeks at a time. When the great D.W. Griffith masterpieces were released in the First World War, there was no West End cinema which fulfilled these criteria. The answer was to hire a legitimate theatre and install projectors in a fire-proof booth for a prolonged run. In this way many West End theatres were converted for the movies and Leicester Square became the hub of London's film world that it still is today.

The London Pavilion in Piccadilly Circus ran a season of film matinees as far back as 1908 and included the 'bioscope' in its regular variety performances. The Scala theatre in Charlotte Street premièred *Birth of a Nation* in 1915, and the cradle of English theatre history, the Theatre Royal, Drury Lane, ran *Intolerance* at full theatre prices in 1917. No doubt theatre managements welcomed an additional lucrative attraction; Covent Garden Opera House, for instance, presented *The Three Musketeers* at the end of 1921 — unthinkable today, but international opera was effectively curtailed by the Great War and for some time afterwards. The

Palace, Cambridge Circus, taken over by the aforementioned Sol Levy from Birmingham in 1920, had a huge hit with *The Four Horsemen of the Apocalypse* in 1922. As we have seen, the Empire and Alhambra in Leicester Square had been experimenting with film since the very beginning.

The first speculative cinema to be built in the West End since the war was the Tivoli in the Strand of 1923. The Tivoli replaced the music hall of the same name, demolished for the widening of the Strand. As the street front of the old Tivoli was lost to the wider thoroughfare, the owners were compensated with a larger site, which had very little depth, being hemmed in by the Royal Society of Arts building at the rear. On this very wide but shallow site, the architects, Bertie Crewe with Gunton and Gunton, managed to squeeze in 2115 seats in stalls and two balconies in a brilliantly simple plan. In theatrical tradition, the proscenium was flanked by stage boxes but they were angled back in a fan formation as at the Regent, Brighton. The Tivoli featured possibly the first auditorium to be influenced by that of the Regent, employing a double and false proscenium in splay configuration with a deep cove between these two elements. This plan had most effectively dealt with the unpleasant 'long hall' appearance of earlier cinemas and solved the problem of blank side walls at the same time. The Tivoli had a most cohesive auditorium, and one confidently expected a substantial stage behind the proscenium. In fact, because of the lack of depth, there was only room for the cinema screen. Access to the two balconies was from a foyer and stair tower on the right hand side, so providing the maximum depth for the auditorium. The Tivoli was leased by MGM in 1925 for an extended run of *Ben Hur*. They went on to lease it for another three years, until their new première house, the rebuilt Empire, Leicester Square, had been completed in 1928. The stage boxes were removed and organ chambers were inserted in one of them by Provincial Cinematograph Theatres in 1928, after that company took over from MGM. The Tivoli suffered an early closure in 1956, killed by the polarisation of films to Leicester Square.

Paramount Pictures hired the London Pavilion in 1923-4, but they went on to become the first Hollywood Studio actually to build their own cinema in London, opening the Plaza, Lower Regent Street, in March 1926. The new cinema formed part of the controversial redevelopment of Regent Street, which had been in progress since before the First World War. The site was excellent, with the entrance on the corner of Jermyn Street, and angled to face Piccadilly Circus, the length of the building running back down Jermyn Street. Their chosen architect, Frank Verity, fresh from his success with the Pavilion, Shepherd's Bush (1923), fitted in nearly 1900 seats in a very compact piece of planning, which included a row of four integral shops on the Regent Street front. The stalls were well below ground level and the right hand access stairs were built under the pavement of Jermyn Street to save valuable space. Externally, Verity provided a chaste exercise in the Palladian style, although with French touches, such as the laurel-filled plaques between the columns on the corner. The Crown Estate, the Regent Street ground landlords, stipulated that the building should be faced with stone. It is one of Verity's most satisfying designs with good proportions and dignity. It was an expensive cinema – the main construction and equipment cost the best part of £400,000 and, with the price of the land, Paramount had to find almost half a million pounds. For the auditorium and foyers, Verity and his decorator Marc Henri turned to the Renaissance style of fifteenth-century Italy, extending it to the design on the safety curtain, which was painted to represent a Florentine fresco, and there was even genuine Italian antique furniture in the foyer. There were two balconies; the lower one, shallow with only three rows of seats, held a mere eighty-four spectators. This somewhat followed the American pattern where a mezzanine level would be placed below

Plaza, Regent Street, London, 1926

the main balcony to gain extra seating and the exclusive location would command higher admission prices. At the Plaza, the depth of the lower balcony was restricted as the main foyer was at this level, ingeniously sandwiched between the ceiling of the rear stalls and the underside of the main balcony. Also revealing an American influence were the splayed ante-proscenium walls (as at the Tivoli).

The Plaza ran 'cine-variety' – films supported by variety acts accompanied by an orchestra, and these acts included the 'Plaza Tiller Girls', twelve chorus girls noted for their precision dancing. The cinema also had one of the new Wurlitzer organs, imported from America. The console in the orchestra pit was the first in

Britain to be placed on an elevator, so that it could rise into view when being played. The Plaza retained an organist right up to closure in 1967, when it was converted into twin cinemas. This obliteration robbed us of one of the showplaces of London.

Around this time Verity was joined in partnership by Samuel Beverley and they became permanent consulting architects to Paramount, designing cinemas for the company in British provincial cities in the next decade, as well as London sisters for the Plaza, the first of which was the Carlton in the Haymarket. This was smaller and decoratively less opulent than the Plaza, but otherwise the planning was similar and some of the details, such as the light fittings, were identical. However, boxes and a deep stage were provided and it opened with a live production, *Lady Luck*, in April 1927. Paramount did not show films in the Carlton until almost a year later when they ran their war flying epic, *Wings*. The coming of the talkies forced live shows out of the Carlton altogether and, but for a few weeks in 1960, the lavish stage facilities and dressing rooms were never used again. The stage house was finally taken down half a century later. Apart from this loss and despite 'tripling' in 1978, the rest of the building has fared better than the Plaza; the Adam-style foyer and substantial elements of the upper half of the original auditorium survive until this day. Its other London sister cinema, the Paramount, Tottenham Court Road, did not appear until 1936.

Frank Verity collaborated with the French architect Auguste Bluysen to design Paramount's cinema in Paris too, which opened in November 1927. Here, the interior combined classical style with motifs derived from the Arts Décoratifs exhibition held in Paris two years earlier, and magnificent art-deco glass fountains stood against the walls flanking the stage.

But by far the largest attempt at dominating London's West End cinema scene by a Hollywood studio was the rebuilding of Thomas Verity's Empire, Leicester Square in 1928. For a full description of the Empire see page 50.

Plaza, Regent Street, London, 1926

The Empire, Leicester Square, London 1928

Architect: Thomas Lamb

The history of entertainment at the Empire, Leicester Square, reaches back to the mid-nineteenth century when 'tableaux vivants' were presented in a mansion on the site. The first Empire opened in 1884 and it became the pre-eminent music hall of late Victorian and Edwardian days. As we have seen in Chapter 1, the Lumière brothers' films were presented at the old Empire in 1896. The Empire was acquired by Jury-Metro-Goldwyn (the British arm of MGM) in 1925, with the intention of redeveloping it as a 'showcase' cinema for their films. The old Empire closed in January 1927 and the new cinema opened in November 1928.

The owners wanted a grand movie palace in the American style, so property adjacent to the existing site had to be acquired to accommodate the new, larger Empire. To achieve the desired grandeur, the design was entrusted to Thomas Lamb, the Scottish-born architect who had designed many important cinemas for Loew's Inc., MGM's parent company in the United States. The façade resembled Lamb's Albee cinema in Cincinnati, and the richly encrusted interior was typical of his other work in the USA. Much of the supervision and structural design was carried out by F. G. M. Chancellor, of Frank Matcham's practice.

Behind the fine Venetian-arched main façade which survives to this day, was the magnificent double-height foyer, lined with mirrors, with stairs in the centre leading down to an inner foyer and the stalls. Two flanking flights ascended to an upper lobby with a huge looking-glass above a false chimney-piece. From here the enormous balcony was reached through a luxuriously decorated tea lounge. Everywhere were crystal chandeliers, rich drapery, ornate Renaissance decoration and carpets to wade through. The opulence must have been almost overpowering. Of its type, the interior of the Empire was unequalled in Britain. Naturally, such luxuries as full stage facilities, a vast Wurlitzer organ and an elevating orchestra pit were also provided. The Empire could seat an audience of 3226, the largest capacity auditorium of any description in the West End. The Empire, of course, had the pick of the product from MGM, the most glittering Hollywood studio, including films starring the worshipped Greta Garbo – both *Queen Christina* and

Camille achieved over 70,000 admissions in their first week of presentation. The stage came into its own in 1949-52 when lavish shows were presented to accompany the films. This was the last flowering of cine-variety on the grand scale.

By the late 1950s it was beginning to be difficult to fill the Empire. In 1961-2 the interior was gutted to create a ballroom in the former stalls area with a new Empire cinema above, one of the last works of the veteran cinema designer George Coles. Coles's cavernous auditorium remains today and, while it is only serviceable compared to what it replaced, it does, nevertheless, have the feel of an old-time movie palace. The rising contour festoon curtain still provides a touch of glamour.

Foyer of the Empire, Leicester Square, 1928

Empire, Leicester Square, London, 1928

9: 'You ain't heard nothing yet!'

This famous dictum, uttered by Al Jolson in *The Jazz Singer*, a film which profoundly changed the face of film production, occurred as an ad-lib by the charismatic vaudeville performer unused to the circumscribed world of movie acting; let alone a technical experiment promoted by one of the smaller Hollywood studios taking a risk with 'talkies'. Spotting spontaneity, the director retained the phrase in the finished picture, thereby christening a byword for sound films to this day.

The genesis of talking pictures takes us back to 1889, when William Dickson demonstrated to Thomas Edison his embryonic Kinetoscope synchronised with his master's previous success, the phonograph, with the words 'Good Morning, Mr Edison, I hope you are satisfied with the Kineto-phonograph!' However, the Kinetoscope was launched as a silent venture, as the sound quality was too poor for commercial exploitation. Experiments with the principle of film sound-track as we know it today (sound waves converted into a printed strip down one side of the film by means of photo-electric cells, and then reproduced in the cinema), were originated by Eugène Augustin Lauste, a former Edison collaborator. Lauste had combined projection equipment developed by

William Friese-Greene in England with theories on sound and light acquired from a German scientist, Ruhmer. His projector was an ad-lib by the charismatic sound-track by 1906, but no large audience could hear them, as he had no way of amplifying the sound. Lauste was unable to apply his invention, but in 1923 Dr Lee De Forest demonstrated a similar system in New York, having solved the audibility problem with his 'audion amplifier'. However, when Warner Brothers were searching for a way of getting ahead of their competitors, they turned to mechanical synchronisation, rather than the photo-electric sound-on-film process. Warner's 'Vitaphone' used large grooved discs, looking very like LP records of recent memory, built into the lower part of the projector, and the first performance before a paying audience took place in the former Piccadilly Theatre on Broadway on 7 August 1926. The show opened with a short talk on film by Will Hays (later a notorious film censor), but disappointingly, all that had been done was to arrange a special orchestral accompaniment to the feature film *Don Juan*, which the critics panned as being a cheap substitute for a live orchestra. *The Jazz Singer* was released just over a year later in October 1927. It too had been produced as a silent, but it was Warner's intention to have the songs in synchronised sound. Jolson was heard singing *Dirty Hands, Dirty Face* and the more famous *Blue Skies*. The film was a huge success, largely because of the personality of Jolson which became evident during the sound interpolations.

With the arrival of the talkies many Broadway actors saw their chance, as did legions of voice coaches and elocutionists; but the clumsy sound-recording equipment slowed up the action and many productions of those early years were plodding indeed, as satirised in the film musical of the 1950s, *Singin' in the Rain*. Meanwhile, the exhibitor and studio owner William Fox had come out with his own system, Movietone, a sound-on-film system, which could be used outside the studio and therefore immediately lent itself as a news-reel medium. One of its earliest coups was footage of Lindbergh's 'The Spirit of St Louis' taking off to cross the Atlantic in May 1927. Coincidentally, Warner chose the Piccadilly Theatre in London for its British première of *The Jazz Singer*, as they had no permanent cinema of their own in London at that time. This sensation reached London on 27 September 1928, and the sequel, *The Singing Fool*, opened at the new Regal, Marble Arch, two months later. The Regal was also the scene of the trade showing of the first British talkie, Alfred Hitchcock's *Blackmail*, in 1929.

At first there was suspicion in the film trade that talkies were a nine-day wonder and would not last. But soon it was realised that they were here to stay, and cinemas were faced with the choice of 'wiring for sound' as quickly as possible, or closure, an inevitability for many smaller cinemas. From this time on, acoustic engineering became an important part of cinema design, as it was necessary to break up flat wall surfaces to reduce echo. Later, so called 'acoustic paints' were introduced to produce a textured surface which helped to 'dry' out the resonance, as did acoustic panelling fitted to the rear walls of auditoria. Domes let into the ceiling also caused havoc with sound but exhibitors thought they gave elegance and dignity to an auditorium, and their more compliant architects continued to specify domes in their plans.

As Hollywood so much dominated the movies, British audiences at first found difficulty with American accents. However, they became accustomed to this, and it was certainly an improvement on the days of subtitles. A recollection passed to the author some years ago was of a young girl brought up in the working-class district near Euston station in London. She told of how, in silent days, the local Tolmer cinema would be a mass of whispering voices – literate children conveying the subtitles to their illiterate parents and grandparents.

Sound film also finally brought to an end the era of the hand-cranked projector. The sound-on-film system required an unvarying speed of projection which only a motor could provide.

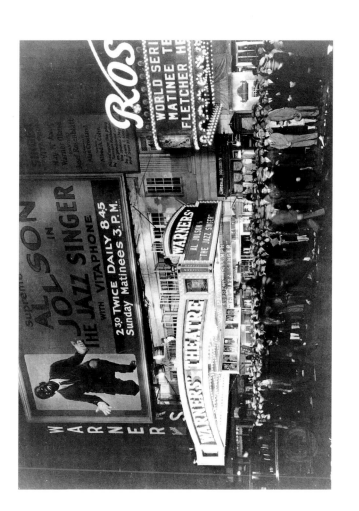

Warners' cinema, New York, showing *The Jazz Singer*, 1927

The Wall Street financial crash came in 1929. In America there were cinemas left uncompleted, or closed down altogether. Some of the many organs which were repossessed ended up in Britain. The construction of new cinemas in the USA began to tail off after 1930. The halcyon years for the USA had been between 1926 and 1929, when a major movie palace was constructed in every city or town of any size. Building continued throughout the 1930s and into the 1940s, but the scale of the cinemas was reduced from capacities in the multi-thousands down to an average of between 800 and 1700 seats. The arrival of the talkies was well timed, rekindling interest before the Depression could take its toll on admissions.

In Britain there had been a moratorium on inessential building construction during the First World War, and it had taken exhibitors most of the decade after the end of the war to realise that it was possible to regularly fill a large cinema of 2000- or 3000-seat capacity and to generally catch up with American developments. As we have seen, there were exceptions, such as the Pavilion, Shepherd's Bush, in London and the Piccadilly in Manchester, but generally buildings of this magnitude had to wait until after 1925 to be realised. In the West End of London, the Hollywood studio

'showcase' cinemas led the way, followed by the only British exhibitor to be building in the 1920s on American lines, Provincial Cinematograph Theatres. Even their development had to mark time until towards the close of the decade.

The PCT company wished to repeat the success of their Regent cinema in Brighton. The architect of the Regent, Robert Atkinson, does not appear to have been re-employed by the company, as their permanent architectural consultant, William Edward Trent, took over to design five large projects, at Sheffield, Preston, Bournemouth, Stamford Hill in north London (with his son, William Sidney Trent) and Hanley, all opening between 1927 and 1929. All were named Regent except the Preston cinema, which was known as the New Victoria. For a sixth Regent, at Bristol (1928), they brought in Percy Bartlett from the office of a respected local architect, William Henry Watkins. The influence on the Regents from America via Atkinson is most obvious in the form of the Bristol Regent, with its semi-elliptical proscenium and pronounced splay plan. This proscenium composition was tied in with the ceiling through an all-embracing saucer dome, decorated with a coffered frieze. Atkinson's festive painted double proscenium was

Green's Playhouse, Glasgow, Scotland, 1927

also repeated. Art deco crept in on the splay walls with the familiar fountain motif. The Bristol Regent was lost in the Second World War bombing raids.

A semi-circular proscenium is very elegant, but it visually conflicts with the shape of the film screen and also, to a certain extent, it constricts its size. It was done away with by Trent at Brighton, when the stage was remodelled in 1929 after a fire, and from then on the more practical squared-off opening was specified for most PCT projects. The auditorium of the Regent at Hanley was to be no exception, though in every other particular it followed a similar formula to that of the Bristol cinema – a saucer dome in the ceiling

with a central opening and neo-classical motifs, but here the splay plan was less pronounced and arcades were introduced to animate the side walls. William Evans, who controlled PCT by the late 1920s, considered himself 'aesthetically aware', having attended art school in his youth. He appears to have been very keen on domed ceilings in his cinemas, as witness his insistence on one for the unique design of the New Victoria in London (see page 84). They added a certain dignity to an interior but could create acoustic problems after sound films were introduced. At Hanley, art deco was introduced to front the organ screens, but also, and most effectively, in the etched and sand-blasted plate-glass interior doors. Somehow

PCT's successors, the Rank Organisation, seemed to forget the Regent, Hanley in its modernisation programme, so it is consequently now a precious survivor. It lies closed at the time of writing but it does have listed status, which guards against summary demolition. Internally, the Bournemouth Regent has been altered out of all recognition, while the Sheffield and Stamford Hill cinemas have been demolished. Trent also completed two more smaller Regents for PCT, at Dudley (1928) and Ipswich (1929), both of which still stand, respectively, as a bingo club and as a rare British example of a cinema becoming a performing arts venue. Both buildings are of the 'stadium' type, where there is no overhanging balcony; a cheaper planning option which precludes the huge and expensive steel balcony main beam. The Ipswich example has a line of boxes ranged along the rear wall of the stalls, an idea possibly derived from Matcham's London Coliseum, and repeated by Trent at the New Victoria cinema in Edinburgh a year later. In February 1929 PCT merged with the Gaumont-British Picture Corporation.

If no other exhibitor was building large-scale cinemas nationally in the second half of the 1920s, then several local concerns were, at least, thinking in terms of very large cinemas. The most spectacular in scale was the vast Green's Playhouse in Glasgow, built between 1925 and 1927. George Green began building up a circuit before 1910 in the early days of the travelling showmen. He built up a small chain in the city and its suburbs, but in order to ensure access to the best films first, he required a cinema in the entertainment heart of Glasgow. His architect, John Fairweather, was despatched to the USA to inspect the latest developments, although it is difficult to detect American influences in his work. Fairweather, or perhaps his patron, was fond of overbearing classical colonnades marching down the side walls of the auditorium, which he used at the Playhouse in Glasgow and again at its sister cinema of the same name in Dundee, built nine years later. At Glasgow, double-banked boxes were marshalled between the columns and although they must have provided a poor view of the screen, the prestige of box seating made them the most expensive seats in the house at three shillings each. Fairweather's plans were approved by the city authorities in September 1925, but this enormous building took two full years to construct at a time when cinemas were often constructed in a year or less. The site was at the top of Renfield Street, opposite the Pavilion variety theatre, and the entrance foyer reused a nineteenth-century row building, connected at the rear to the auditorium block. The stalls were at basement level and were 'dished' to create a 'reverse rake' at the stage end. The first balcony was approached through a large tearoom; the front rows accommodated what Green dubbed the 'Golden Divan' seats, while further

back were the 'Red Divans'; a clever marketing strategy which made this premium seating famous throughout Scotland. Above, was a second balcony stretching up into the heavens and, while the view of the auditorium from here must have been spectacular, the 1927 'Academy ratio' screen must have appeared like a small dot of light at the end of a very long tunnel.

The total seating capacity at the time of opening was said to be 4254, making it the largest cinema in Europe until the Gaumont Palace in Paris opened in 1931 with something approaching 6000 seats. Above this towering auditorium were administrative offices, possibly built as a sound baffle, for higher still was a ballroom rising another two storeys. To fully appreciate the sheer scale of this complex it was instructive to walk around the outside into West Nile Street where the back of the Playhouse reared up ten storeys and resembled nothing more than the exterior of a utilitarian power station. Another adjacent Victorian building on this site was annexed to make a block of dressing rooms. A stage was provided but it was less than twenty feet deep. Green appears to have had difficulty in filling all those seats every day and competition must have become tougher after the more modern Paramount cinema opened further down Renfield Street in 1934. The Playhouse closed in 1973, the upper balcony having been abandoned years before. The cinema, by then very run down, was refurbished to become a rock venue, but this too failed and Glasgow's most spectacular showplace is now only a memory.

Another Scottish exhibitor thinking along similar lines was Maguire and Lumley, which promoted the largest cinema Edinburgh was ever to have, also named Playhouse, and situated in Leith Walk on the north side of the city. The partners in the project made a fact-finding tour of the USA, and on their return hired Fairweather to design the cinema, which opened in 1929. The building presents a low, unexceptional façade to Leith Walk, but it is like the top of an iceberg, as the land falls away sharply towards the rear, with the result that the bulk of it lies below street level. This constructional difficulty aside, Fairweather had an easier site to deal with here in that it was more or less square, rather than the long rectangular shape of Green's in Glasgow. He produced a double-tier solution, very much in the theatre tradition, with seating for 3053. There was a deep stage, an organ and an orchestra pit elevator – the 'Playhouse Rising Orchestra' became something of a local institution during the 1930s. Problems filling the Playhouse only came with the general downturn of admissions in the 1960s, when being an 'independent' aggravated the situation as the major circuit houses in the city had first call on the most commercial films. The author remembers being pleased to find *Bridge over the River*

Kwai reissued at the Playhouse on a first visit to the northern capital in 1970. The audience appeared very sparse in so vast an auditorium, and the balcony was almost deserted – the upper tier would almost certainly have been out of use by that date. It was then a great and dignified movie palace in decline, but it is a joy that the future of this magnificent building is assured as a 'lyric' theatre – especially useful during the Edinburgh Festival each year.

In Croydon, south London, once stood a further 1920s giant, the Davis cinema. The last of the projects built by the Israel Davis circuit, it was retained by the company after they shed their other properties to Gaumont in 1927. The Davis opened a year later in December 1928, and was the work of one of the better known specialist cinema architects, Robert Cromie. The Davis had seats for an audience of 3725 and was arranged on three levels, the shallow mezzanine balcony pretentiously named the 'Royal' circle. Access was through a rotunda foyer some sixty feet in diameter, connected to the auditorium block. A restaurant occupied the upper level which had a continuous balcony enabling diners to look down on the audience waiting for admission. Decoratively, the interior was a fusion of the classical and art deco, described at the time as 'modern French'. The least successful aspect of the design was the marrying together of the arched and chamfered proscenium with the classically ordered flank walls; because Cromie's auditoria tended to be angular with flat ceilings, a squared-off opening might well have better solved the problem. Likewise, Cromie's balconies at the Davis were set too far back making even the front seats remote from the

stage. However, the detailing and wall surfaces were superb, with wonderful art-deco light fittings. A seat towards the rear of the upper balcony made it much easier to inspect these, although the screen was somewhat distant. There was a large stage and the Davis was in continuous use for opera, ballet and orchestral performances as well as for films; the inaugural concert by the Royal Philharmonic Orchestra took place there in 1946 and the Bolshoi Ballet visited ten years later. The theatre was demolished in 1959, a victim of television and the enormous profits to be made from redeveloping the site during the Croydon office-building boom years in the wake of the London decentralisation scheme. To their credit, the district authority reinvested some of the increased rates into the construction of a new concert hall which satisfied a local need, but a replacement cinema was not apparently considered necessary. The Davis disappeared years before its architectural interest could have been recognised and the council rejected the organ (which had, by then, it has to be admitted, lost its popular appeal) for installation in the new hall. What makes the Davis such a tragic loss is that there was a real need in Croydon for a performing arts venue and it was only demolished because it appeared architecturally passé at the time. Initially, the Davis was such a success that the owners were keen to repeat this scheme elsewhere. They found a suitable site in Hammersmith, west London, and had Cromie draw up plans, but the scheme was taken over by Gaumont and the cinema opened under their auspices in 1932 (see Chapter 17).

Regent, Bournemouth, Hampshire, 1929

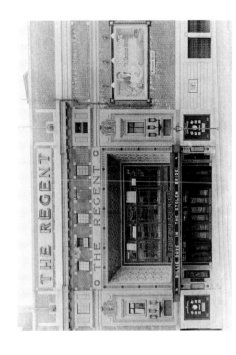

Regent, Sheffield, West Yorkshire, 1927

Joseph Mears had established a small but profitable circuit in west London. He was an enlightened client and employed the highly regarded architect and critic, Julian Rudolph Leathart (1891-1978) with his partner W.F. Granger, to design four picture houses between 1926 and 1930. The first was the Kensington which opened in 1926 (now the Odeon, Kensington). The auditorium was a conventional straight-sided hall with a balcony, but with much neo-classical decoration. From this point of view it could have been designed ten years earlier, but the main interest of the building lies in the striking façade (which survives basically untouched) and in the quality of the materials used. This façade is of unusual dignity, an improved version of Atkinson's façade for the Regent, Brighton, repeating the 'proscenium' theme, with a row of entrance doors and a screen of windows above, recessed behind a monolithic arch. It was expected that this configuration would entice audiences inside a great welcoming orifice, although no provision was made for the film publicity. The entrance hall displayed a conspicuous use of marble, complete with a copy of the Portland vase standing in the centre. On either side, 'imperial' stairs rose to the various balcony levels. These are still in situ although no other vestige of

the interior has been allowed to survive. It is doubtful that this austere approach was appropriate for an entertainment building, but it did proclaim the respectability of film in a middle-class district – an important function at a time when cinema was trying to rid itself of its fairground image. It also, however, indicates an architect searching for new architectural formulae, and Leathart's next project for Mears, the Twickenham of 1928, was another essay in innovation.

The Twickenham was praised by that most acerbic of architectural writers, P. Morton Shand, in his polemical book of 1930, *The Architecture of Pleasure: Modern Theatres and Cinemas*. He described the cinema as 'by far the best façade which any English cinema yet built can boast, and one of the few that can sustain comparison with current Continental examples'. Julian Leathart is named as 'our foremost cinema architect' and Shand's caption to the picture of the Twickenham states, 'An encouraging example of English Modernism, slightly over-detailed', and then 'The wrought-iron fillings of the triple opening above the marquise do not seem very happily or surely designed' – a carping and unnecessary remark. But to quote Robert Elwall in *The Dreamlands of Julian Leathart*, 'What Shand

Twickenham cinema, Surrey, 1928

Richmond cinema, Surrey, 1929

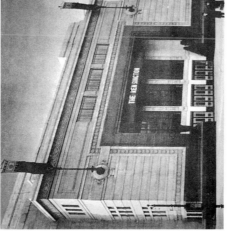

Kensington cinema, west London, 1926

found too elaborate … the good citizens of Twickenham complained was too severe. Locals lost no time in expressing horror at the large unbroken wall surfaces and the virtual elimination of ornament inside and out. "Mears has put up an atrocious cinema at Twickenham; when you go in it is like a bare barn. I prefer the one up the road, the Luxor", opined a local colonel's wife.' To this correspondent, Leathart testily replied in the *RIBA Journal* of December 1950, that 'an elevation need not necessarily be decked with bunches of bananas tied with twisted ribbon, interspersed with flambeaux, masks and olive wreaths to express a place of entertainment'. The plain rendered façade relieved by the triple openings, the crenellated parapet with geometrical designs and pantiled flanking roofs added up to something Moorish, worthy of an Eberson 'atmospheric' *interior*. In old photographs the cinema appears to be completely anonymous, with no name appearing anywhere on the street façade. So often architects made no provision for advertising or graphics, with the result that these elements, designed by others, could detract from the original concept. The Twickenham came down in 1956.

While Leathart and Granger appeared to be unconsciously leaning towards vernacular Spain with the exterior of the Twickenham, the auditorium of their next commission, the Richmond Cinema, gave full rein to this inclination, designing it, according to contemporary publicity, to represent 'the courtyard of a seventeenth-century Spanish nobleman's house'. In some respects this indicates a radical change of direction for this practice, although in the search for something new they could well have been influenced by their client who, no doubt, would have desired the latest craze imported from America. The Richmond was being designed in 1929 when cinemas in the 'atmospheric' style were first appearing in Britain, with much advance publicity in the trade press. Julian Leathart was to denounce the style only five years later, realising that the fad was short-lived and had dated very quickly. Morton Shand was appalled by the Richmond, accusing Leathart of going 'over to the enemy' and quoting another commentator's phrase decrying the interior as 'architecturalised acoustics'. With hindsight we can appreciate the Richmond interior as being one of the most successful in a semi-atmospheric mode, for while there is much Mediterranean foliage and a clear plaster 'sky' onto which lighting effects were projected by the new 'Holophane' system, the 'buildings' were symmetrical and the metal-work grilles flanking the stage are inspired by art deco. Elsewhere in the building there is high quality detail in the elaborately carved doors (some of them now sadly painted over), and plaster panels in Aztec style depicting boats, said to have been requested by Mears because of one of his

other business interests — River Thames pleasure steamers. The Richmond, like all Mears's cinemas, was taken over by the Odeon group in 1944. It passed to Rank, who have not given the interior the special attention it deserves, but it is at least open for films and is, by reputation, still a highly profitable operation.

The last cinema Leathart and Granger designed for Joseph Mears, the Sheen (1930), in East Sheen, a suburban area barely two miles from Richmond, was the most innovative, at least as far as the main façade was concerned. Here, the architects seemed to be solving their quest for a new image. There were few classical allusions, although the façade was strictly symmetrical with sculpted reliefs in jade-green faience (by Eric Aumonier) supporting a vertical protrusion which carried the name of the cinema and was glazed to become a tower of light after dark. Surmounting this was a triple urn feature, illuminated from behind, which therefore appeared in a halo of light. Contrasting bands of faience enlivened the ground-floor level and below the main cornice. From this façade we can deduce that Leathart was aware of Swedish contemporary architecture and of the latest developments in 'night architecture' from Germany, later to be extensively employed by the architects for the Odeon cinemas. The Sheen received high praise from Morton Shand, who wrote that it could 'hold its own with anything so far done abroad' adding that he had 'never seen a better night elevation in any foreign country'. The cinema was completed in late 1930 and the composition of its frontage should be placed alongside Wamsley Lewis's almost exactly contemporary New Victoria, London, and the little known reworking of the Bear Street façade of the Cameo, Charing Cross Road, by Robert Atkinson in 1926, in that they were all breaking new ground and eschewing direct classical references, which had until then been prevalent in cinema design. The auditorium was restrained and confident in the same vein. All the lighting was indirect, being housed in coves in the ceiling and in niches at the top of the side walls. The Sheen became a model for the medium-sized super cinema of 1930s suburbs; it demonstrated how to use brick with stone or faience in a way which would fit in well with suburban High Streets, and yet be a striking advertisement for the movies. It had consummate taste both internally and externally. The secluded suburban environment of this cinema proved to be its undoing, as by the 1960s every household in the district probably had a television set, and there was also a premium on sites large enough on which to build a supermarket. Therefore the Sheen is no more. The Sheen was Leathart and Granger's penultimate cinema scheme; subsequently there was only to be the Dreamland, Margate, in 1935 (another revolutionary design, see page 93), before the partnership was dissolved in 1937.

Sheen cinema, Surrey, 1930

12: George Coles: A Versatile Architect and His Great London Cinemas

George Coles, the most versatile of cinema architects, sometimes described as 'the English Thomas Lamb', was responsible for a spectacular series of projects for H & G Kinemas. The names behind this anonymous appellation were the entrepreneurial Hyams brothers and a Major Arthur Gale.

The Broadway, Stratford, east London, opened in 1927. With 2768 seats it was Coles's largest cinema to date and was a huge public success. The entrance front was clad in faience although the flanking screen walls with shops on the ground floor were only in brick. The long, low auditorium was in Coles's neo-classical early taste. A more exciting scheme was his Metropole, opposite Victoria Station in central London, of 1929. In fact, the Metropole was instigated by another operator and Coles transferred with the project when the Hyams took control. A façade dominated by a Venetian window lit an elegant foyer, with a tea lounge on the first floor. Beyond, the impressive Spanish Renaissance auditorium, decorated in amber, gold and blue, was constructed at right angles to the entrance. An entirely successful conception, only the foyer block survives today, but most of its original decoration is intact. A year later, on 22 December 1930, what was arguably Coles's

greatest interior in the classical mould appeared at that hub of Cockneys life south of the Thames, the Elephant & Castle. Here, numerous tram routes from over the river converged, fanning out again to serve outlying suburbs. With two Underground lines, a surface railway station and numerous bus routes passing the doors, the Trocadero, named after the expensive Shaftesbury Avenue restaurant, was bound to be a gold mine, and until the London County Council decided to comprehensively redevelop the area in the early 1960s, it was just that. The Trocadero was a difficult building to plan, as it had to take into account a subtle bend in the road causing the left-hand wing to break the symmetry of the façade. The site was almost square and in order to pack in 3594 people, Coles turned the axis of the plan onto the diagonal, thereby creating a wide, fan-shaped auditorium. So tight was the planning that foyer spaces had to be kept to a minimum. His masterly solution of the awkward junction where the high auditorium walls and the ceiling met was dealt with in the manner of Thomas Lamb, with wide niches brought to a peak within the main cove. American influence was present, not only in the planning and configuration of the design, but also in the density of the Renaissance decoration. Coles

Foyer of the Troxy, Stepney, east London, 1933

would have been aware of the recently completed new Empire in Leicester Square in the West End, with a genuine Lamb interior and, as Dennis Sharp put it, 'the Troc [as it became affectionately known] brought three hours of Piccadilly luxury and comfort to the patron for the price of a big sandwich'. The three hours would be filled with two feature films, a newsreel, a stage show and an interlude on the largest Wurlitzer organ in Europe. If the Trocadero had to go, it could not have been more honourably replaced than in the form of Ernö Goldfinger's Odeon in 1966, but even this is now a thing of the past.

Looking to repeat the success of the Trocadero, the Hyams brothers investigated another inner-London working-class district, Stepney, and on Commercial Road, in August 1933, the Troxy opened, the name obviously derived from a combination of the Trocadero and the Roxy, New York, which had become a byword for the luxury cinema. Here Coles, a keen devotee of faïence, employed that material on a channelled 'proscenium' façade, producing a version of Leathart's Kensington front. Internally, however, Coles went for full-blown French-inspired art deco and this was possibly his richest essay in this style, so different from the streamlined modernistic cinemas he would design for the Odeon group just a few years later. Fortunately, most of this high-quality decoration survived during the twenty-five years from around 1960 when the cinema was used as a rehearsal and scene-building workshop by the Covent Garden Opera House. The Troxy is now listed, partially restored and is in use for bingo.

Coles's largest project for H & G Kinemas was the Gaumont State, Kilburn, in north-west London. Originally also to have been named the Troxy, the cinema came under Gaumont control before opening in 1937. See page 90 for a detailed survey of the Gaumont State.

Trocadero, Elephant & Castle, south London, 1930

The year was 1928 and the race was on for the first 'atmospheric' cinema to open in Britain. It was announced that the Alhambra, Balsall Heath, Birmingham, would win this prize, but it was beaten by the opening on 1 October 1928 of the Lido at Golders Green in north London. The architect was W.J. King, and the auditorium, painted to represent a scene on a north-Italian lake, was executed by Guy Lipscombe. But apart from fake belfries flanking the stage to accommodate the organ, the interior of the Lido was merely paint applied to plaster, without the elaborate three-dimensional structures of the American originals. Lighting was from a shallow dome in the ceiling, making a nonsense of the 'sky'. The Alhambra, when it opened three months later, was even less convincing, with landscapes only appearing as panels on the side walls.

We divert at this point to a very attractive aberration, much publicised as an 'atmospheric' before its opening in November 1928, but in reality a return to the winter-garden idea of the proto-'atmospherics', as exemplified by the theatre of the same name in Toronto and the Cort in Chicago. The Regal, Marble Arch, London, had scenes on the auditorium walls depicting woodland settings, while the ceiling comprised a pergola festooned with creeper and vine leaves, together with more fake foliage cascading down in front of the organ screens. The theme was by no means consistent, with allusions to the ancient history of the site in the form of Roman tripods appearing between garlanded glades, and an almost art-deco star-burst above the proscenium. The architect was Clifford Aish, with Charles Muggeridge as decorator. This preposterous but very sumptuous interior was lost when the cinema was demolished after closure in 1964. The Majestic, Wembley, which opened in January 1929, designed by J. Field and H.J. Stewart, with an interior by W.E. Greenwood, was approaching a more authentic 'atmospheric'. Here, at least, was a clear ceiling onto which atmospheric effects could be projected from floodlights in the balcony front, but, again, much of the decoration depended on mere paint, and the scale of the interior was too small for this to be much of a success. A more successful 'atmospheric' interior was created by W.E. Greenwood for the Savoy, Dublin, in the same year.

But the finest examples of true 'atmospheric' genre in Britain, where there was a budget sufficient to create the architectural effects, were the two Astoria cinemas in the populous Victorian suburbs of Brixton in south London and Finsbury Park, north of the

Regal, Marble Arch, London, 1928

Thames. The same team of architect and decorators was responsible for both these cinemas, respectively Edward A. Stone, and Thomas Somerford with Ewen Barr. Stone was an established cinema and theatre architect whose work in the field dated back to before the First World War; Somerford had been responsible for many London billiard halls, and Barr was also designing the Duchess Theatre in the West End at that time. Externally, neither cinema could be admired, consisting of huge inelegant brick façades with faience dressings in debased classical style on the entrance frontages. But Stone's planning was excellent and in the case of the Finsbury Park Astoria, most ingenious. These two 'atmospheric' interiors were among the most successful of their type outside America. They were promoted by a company (whose chairman was also Edward Stone), which had obtained backing from Paramount, necessary for the colossal investment in such huge buildings. There were two other less ambitious Astorias, built at Streatham (only a couple of miles south of Brixton) and Bermondsey (Old Kent Road), but these could not boast such extravagant interiors. All four were completed between August 1929 and September 1930 and between them provided 11,259 seats for the capital.

The Brixton Astoria opened first, and was the largest with nearly 5000 seats, although the publicity, as ever, exaggerated this figure to 4500. All the Astorias had generous standing areas so the actual capacity was greater than the number of seats. Entry was, and remains, through a circular outer lobby and into a double-height stair hall, beyond which the vast fan-shaped auditorium is reached. Somerford and Barr's scheme represents a gigantic Italian courtyard with an Ionic colonnade at stalls level, its entablature cleverly continuing into the balcony front, the style becoming more relaxed higher up with poplars rising in front of a horizon. The scheme had all the best attributes of Eberson's interiors – sufficient scale and asymmetrical two-dimensional 'buildings'. Above was the great curved plaster sky, while a loggia was arranged over the stage, on which automatic figures are said to have moved. Here was literally 'An Acre of Seats in a Garden of Dreams', to quote American publicity for similar creations.

At the Finsbury Park Astoria, the last to be completed, Stone was faced with the planning problem of how to connect his entrance hall block, on a corner facing a busy main road and a railway station, with the huge auditorium which lay to the rear of Victorian terraced houses. This he solved in a brilliant plan in which the transition from one area to another is achieved imperceptibly. The auditorium style has been described as a 'Hispano-Mooresque fantasy' and is arguably even more ambitious than its Brixton sister; cupolas, turrets and loggias vie with one another for attention and

Astoria, Brixton, south London, 1929

the great semi-circular stage opening supports a Spanish baroque pediment of awesome dimensions. Below, gilded lions guarded the stage from atop giant twisted barley-sugar columns. By the 1970s, both these dream palaces were far too large to be economic as cinemas and they were converted into live-music venues, a use which continues to this day at Brixton. At Finsbury Park, however, the Astoria waits for some rich Prince Charming to reawaken its glistening attractions. Although both are now very run down, they are highly regarded and are listed grade II*. No greater 'atmospherics' appeared in Britain and it is now necessary to visit the Rex cinema in Paris to experience the full magnificence of an 'atmospheric' in daily use for film performances.

The 'atmospheric' craze was short-lived, for although in America this type of cinema was considered cheap to build, in Britain they were an expensive option. Around twelve 'atmospherics' were built altogether in Britain, but none matched up to the Astorias in Brixton and Finsbury Park. Two more rather second-rate examples were perpetrated by W. E. Greenwood at Staines (1929) and High Wycombe (1930) and in Glasgow there were 'atmospheric' interiors at the Toledo, Muirend, and the Orient, Gallowgate. The best of this subsidiary group was the Avenue cinema constructed in North-field Avenue, Ealing, west London, in 1932. Here the intended effect was that of a Spanish thoroughfare, with a festively striped

Astoria, Brixton, south London, 1929

Foyer of the Astoria, Finsbury Park, north London, 1930

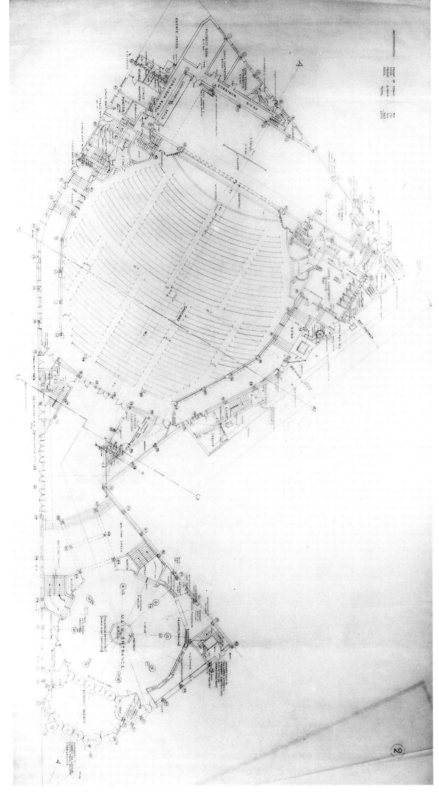

Plan of the Astoria, Finsbury Park, north London, 1930

Avenue, Ealing, west London, 1932

Palace, Southall, west London, 1929

awning stretched across the street against the glare of the midday sun. Again we have asymmetrical 'buildings' flanking the side walls, heavily textured to represent ancient plaster. The denizens of Ealing obviously suspended their disbelief to accept the presence of a candelabra hanging from the awning. The name 'Avenue' hardly prepared the patron for this exotic interior, and it soon gained a local nickname — 'Spanish City'. The architect was Cecil Masey, who had also designed a little-known 'atmospheric' at Colchester, the Regal, of 1931. In the 1930s, holidays in Italy or Spain were the preserve of the rich, and these interiors were the nearest the average person was likely to get to the romantic and seductive Mediterranean shores. They may look like elaborate kitsch to us now, but they had a psychological appeal and a cathartic effect during the worst of the Depression years.

Unlikely as it was that the great mass of movie-goers would ever visit Spain or Italy, it was even less likely that they would ever go further afield, to Egypt or China, for instance. After the discovery of King Tutankhamun's tomb in 1922, things Egyptian had become fashionable, and the Egyptian style was gaining general architectural currency within the stylistic canon, both as an alternative to the classical vocabulary and because of its monumental properties. We have already touched on how some architects were attuned to the desire of exhibitors to build on the most monolithic scale possible, both in America and Britain — the façade of the Kensington cinema is nothing if not monumental. As architects and their clients were searching for some novel architectural identity, the call of Karnak began to appeal. In the USA, Grauman's Egyptian in Hollywood Boulevard went up in the same year as the Tutankhamun revelations, and others were constructed around the same time, such as the still extant Egyptian cinema in De Kalb, Illinois. But there are earlier examples of the Egyptian style being used for entertainment venues. In his book, *The Picture Palace*, Dennis Sharp illustrates a tantalising Egyptian cinema interior from c.1916. There was also a distinguished antecedent in the form of the Egyptian Hall in Piccadilly, London, of 1811.

The monolithic scale of an Egyptian façade needed to be faced in stone, in preference to brick. Failing costly ashlar, a veneer of faience was an ideal substitute. It was to this material that George Coles turned when designing, in 1928, the front of the Carlton, Upton Park in east London, the most successful Egyptian façade on any British cinema. Conceived as a portico, it had columns with the characteristic bell-shaped lotus-leaf capitals and a concave cornice, above which was a winged scarab. The flat surfaces were in white faience, but the ornament made good use of the colourful possibilities of this material. The Carlton as a cinema was a most

extraordinary concept, for behind the alluring façade there extended a long foyer leading to a huge single-level auditorium fitted into the courtyard of a former nineteenth-century workhouse. Coles's next cinema, also named Carlton, for the same promoters (Albert Clavering and John Rose), in Islington, north London, employed a like formula, although with less success, as the portico theme was hoisted to first-floor level above a standard cinema entrance and canopy, thereby losing much of its impact. The more interesting Upton Park front was damaged in the Second World War and rebuilt in a different form, but the Islington example remains, now in use for bingo, and is listed. Curiously, the Egyptian influence did not extend to the interiors and Coles provided straightforward classical auditoria for both cinemas.

Elsewhere, Egyptian-inspired schemes took off, most notably the Pyramid in Sale (a suburb of Manchester), the work of Joseph Gomersall in 1933, with its double pylon façade incorporating more bell-shaped lotus leaf capitals and with similar motifs used inside. There was even a custom-built organ console in Egyptian style with Pharaoh heads staring down on the audience. The faience façade of the Luxor, Twickenham, 1929, by John Stanley Beard, was also influenced by the style — an example of what John Betjeman labelled 'Egypto-Commercial-Renaissance-cum-Georgian'; the bell-shaped lotus-leaf capitals were there along with stylised winged heads, but otherwise the purity had become blurred. The concern was primarily to create an eye-catching contemporary building to attract an undiscerning audience. Internally, however, the Egyptian theme was much stronger, with a great bird with outstretched wings flying above the stage. Whatever its merits as an example of 'Egyptianising', it is regrettable that the Luxor has now been replaced by a mundane block of flats. In the 1980s it seemed impossible to convince the authorities that it should be preserved. The Luxor was an eccentric oddity, certainly not 'serious' architecture and therefore it had to go. The previously mentioned Astoria, Streatham, also had auditorium decoration inspired by the Egyptian taste. By 1930, the Egyptian style had blended with art deco to create the much derided Jazz Moderne, and this continued to be extensively employed by architects building super cinemas during the next decade.

The use of Chinese motifs was very limited in Britain, although more common in the USA. George Coles despatched his young assistant, Arthur Roberts, to the reading room of the British Museum to gather information for the design of the Chinese-style Palace cinema in Southall. It opened in 1929, and on the pantile pagoda roof were dragons with writhing tails. Even the lettering for the cinema name had a Chinese inflection. Coles once again clothed

Foyer of the Beaufort, Birmingham,
1929

the outside with serviceable glazed faience. Internally, the decoration was more muted, although Chinese lanterns glowed from the ceiling and there were diminutive pagoda roofs above panels in the side walls. The Palace is a listed building but has been converted into a shopping arcade.

The very ethos of life in suburban Birmingham was to reject that great industrial city and aspire to a life in rural Warwickshire, the county of Shakespeare, rich in 'olde worlde' timber-framed houses. When planning a cinema for the suburb of Ward End, the architect Archibald Hurley Robinson realised that hard, industrialised shiny finishes would not be popular, and that something in harmony with the rural idyll was required. To this end, the Beaufort cinema appeared in 1929, looking both internally and externally like something out of Alexander Korda's yet to be made film of Henry VIII. The foyer block was rendered in patent Guildstone, while the auditorium was a riot of fake beams interspersed with plaster panels, and his family desiring to escape from the big city and its toils.

The Tudor revival style was not only popular with the public between the wars, but it could also solve tricky problems in historic areas where the local planning authority could object to anything too modern. Such a place was Salisbury, but here the main difficulty was how to graft a modern cinema onto an existing medieval building. The Gaumont-British Picture Corporation acquired the ancient Hall of John Halle for use as the foyer of their new Gaumont Palace cinema. The hall, restored by A.W.N. Pugin in 1858, had, prior to this novel adaptation, been in use as a porcelain emporium. Notes contained in the brochure issued for the opening in 1931 purport to reveal a philosophy behind the decision to extend the medieval theme into the new cinema: 'after anxious consideration it was agreed that a break from the early work to a theatre designed and treated in the modern manner would be too abrupt and hard … So the theatre has been treated in a manner suggestive of an old fifteenth-century hall with a timber-panelled and plastered ceiling, and stone walls hung with tapestries … a more fitting environment for the romance portrayed on the screen would be difficult to find.' In fact, one suspects that the company's architects, William Trent and Ernest Tulley, saw this 'problem' as a glorious justification for some architectural high jinks. The 'stone' walls were, of course, made of plaster and the 'tapestries' consisted of canvas sheets skil-

fully painted by Frank Barnes (an artist frequently employed by Gaumont-British) to look from a distance like the real thing. Originally there was an elaborate 'medieval' tableau stage curtain which moved aside in one direction only, rather than rising or parting. This Gaumont Palace became part of the Rank empire when the two circuits amalgamated in 1948 and it is still open for films today, although it has been divided into smaller units, a policy which has damaged the unity of the original auditorium. If this had to happen to ensure its survival, one cannot help wondering if it would have been preferable for the city to have acquired the building as a performing arts centre. The Hall of John Halle has been a scheduled ancient monument for many years, but Trent and Tulley's auditorium is now listed in its own right.

bearings and the Tudor rose. Even the paybox inside the entrance was thickly clad with linen-fold panelling. The Beaufort was extended in 1957 onto adjacent land, thereby gaining another 500 seats. It was the dream palace par excellence for middle-class man

The route up to the balcony passed through a hall lit by windows filled with stained glass representing Henry, his wives, armorial

Gaumont Palace, Salisbury, Wiltshire, 1931

In 1931 the ultimate in fantasy cinemas materialised in the south London suburb of Tooting: the Granada, the masterpiece of the Russian designer Theodore Komisarjevsky, was to provide a golden gothic shrine to celluloid. See page 75 for a detailed description of the Granada, Tooting.

The story of Granada cinemas was to start on a walking tour of Andalucia, when the promoter of the Granada chain, Sidney Bernstein, visited the city of the same name. Later, when he was planning a cinema in Dover to be called the County, Bernstein decided this dull and unromantic name should be changed to that of the Spanish city which had so excited him. Furthermore, the name also influenced the decoration, the interior being designed in the Moorish style. The Granada, Dover, opened to much publicity in January 1930, and guests from London travelled down by train in a special Pullman car. The trade paper, *The Bioscope*, described the auditorium as 'having a suggestion of the Alhambra, a Russian ballet dream of Granada rather than an attempted reproduction'. Bernstein and Komisarjevsky are said to have completed some of the painting themselves in a frantic rush to have the cinema ready on time. Sidney Bernstein, later to become Lord Bernstein, had inherited a chain of London cinemas built up by his father before the First World War. He was also a founding member of the Film Society, created to promote the medium as an art form in its own right, and had an interest in the stage. Through friends in the theatre, he was introduced to Theodore Komisarjevksy, and in 1927 they went into partnership to run the Royal Court Theatre in London. After a trip to the USA that year, Bernstein became convinced by the idea of promoting the whole picture-going activity to the public, and the importance of the cinema building itself to the experience. He raised capital by disposing of his interests in his existing properties, and launched into the construction of a new circuit of luxury cinemas, commencing with the Dover venture, and engaging Komisarjevsky as his interior designer.

From then on, all Bernstein's cinemas were to be named Granada and the second one, opening in September 1930 at Walthamstow in north-east London, had a large 2500-seat auditorium in which the Moorish style was even more pronounced than its predecessor. The shell of the building was the work of Cecil Masey, who made a particularly good job of the street front, and who was to work regularly for Bernstein throughout the decade.

**The Granada, Tooting,
south London 1931**
Architect: Cecil Masey
*Interior designer: Theodore
Komisarjevsky*

Completed in 1931, the Granada, Tooting, represents the high point of the extravagant fantasy cinema interior in Britain. It was the third Granada to be built by Sidney Bernstein, who believed that the cinema should be a total fantasy experience – a place to escape from reality and be hypnotised by film in magical surroundings.

To create his temples to film, Bernstein employed Theodore Komisarjevsky who, while he had received an architectural training in Russia, only worked on the Granada interiors. The shell of the Tooting Granada was the responsibility of Cecil Masey, one of Bernstein's regular architects. Masey also designed the main street façade, which has a marked similarity to that of Giles Gilbert Scott's Phoenix Theatre in the West End, completed for the same client in the previous year.

For the Tooting interior, Komisarjevsky raided the textbooks of European gothic architecture – the great portals in the auditorium hint at Rheims Cathedral and Notre Dame in Paris, and the foyer conjures up Walpole's Strawberry Hill. Above the balcony is a richly coffered ceiling from which elaborate gothic candelabra are suspended. Exotic troubadours and wimpled damsels, painted by Vladimir Polunin and Leslie le Blond, gaze down from niches above the loge seats. Furniture dotted around the foyers would not have disgraced Pugin. The architectural critic Ian Nairn wrote, 'Miss the Tower of London if you have to, but don't miss this'. The Granada still survives in almost all its glory, but is now the home of dedicated bingo players. The organ console, however, lies entombed below the bingo caller's platform.

The Granada, Tooting, was one of the first cinemas to be statutorily listed in 1972.

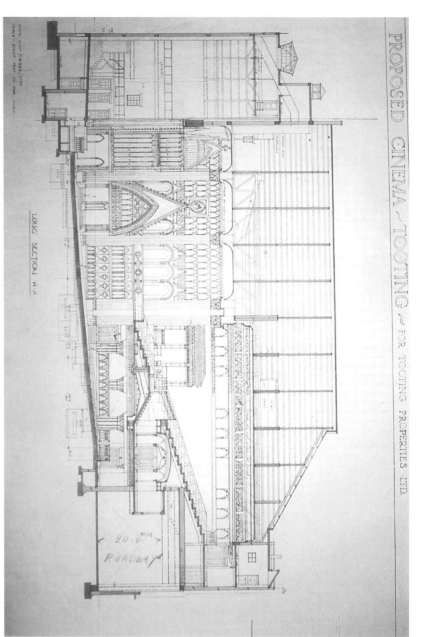

PROPOSED CINEMA ~ TOOTING ~ FOR TOOTING PROPERTIES LTD.

LONG SECTION A-A

Section of the Granada, Tooting, south
London, 1931, by Cecil Masey,
incorporating Theodore Komisarjevsky's
designs

Foyer of the Granada, Tooting, south
London, 1931

Foyer of the Empire, Edmonton, north London, 1933

Granada, Walthamstow, east London, 1930

In 1933 Bernstein reconstructed his father's Empire theatre in Edmonton, north London, originally designed by Masey in 1908. Komisarjevsky's new foyer for the cinema represented a complete break from the lavish historical ornamentation present in his other Granada schemes. The cubistic design of converging structural members painted in primary colours was described at the time as 'ultra-modern' and having 'simplicity and bold colours'. The cinema closed in 1968 and demolition followed soon afterwards.

There were a further fifteen Granadas built between 1934 and 1939, six opening in 1937 alone. They were mainly constructed in the older London suburbs but some appeared in newer districts such as Greenford and North Cheam, the latter in anticipation of a London Underground extension which never materialised. Others were built in existing town centres, such as Kingston and Woolwich, which had by then been engulfed by Greater London. An atypical development was the Granada in Manchester, but this escaped from the pack – shortly before opening in 1935 it was sold to the Gaumont circuit. Now demolished, it was one of the more elaborate examples in the standard Granada Renaissance mode.

Between designing and directing for the stage, and visits to the USA, Komisarjevsky had overall design responsibility for all the Granadas, with the exception of those at Wandsworth Road, just south of the Thames, and Greenwich. The Tooting and the Manchester Granada/Gaumont apart, the most notable in the chain were those at Clapham Junction in south London and at Woolwich, opening within a few months of one another in 1937. Both cinemas had modernistic street fronts, the one at Woolwich by Reginald Uren being particularly dramatic, employing streamlined windows and a neon-lit 'fin' tower. Uren was inspired by the Dutch architect Dudok, but it is likely that both he and Bernstein would have been aware of the success of the fin towers featured on the Odeons being erected at the time; there was an Odeon with a fin tower being built at the same time right opposite the Granada. Internally, however, all was gothic, like at Tooting six years earlier, although problems arose at the collision between Reginald Uren's streamlined façade windows and the gothic fantasy foyer. A Hall of Mirrors led to an elaborate auditorium with many of the same elements as the Tooting Granada, such as the steeply pointed gables over the emergency exit doors on the ante-proscenium walls. Gothic panels cleverly disguised the awkward junction at balcony level where the auditorium widens out. At Clapham a more conventional brick exterior by Cecil Masey with H.R. Horner and Leslie Norton, surrounded a Renaissance interior by Komisarjevsky with complex coffered ceilings and painted panels and friezes.

Of the cinemas opened by Granada, some have been demolished

altogether and others wrecked by later alterations, but most have been converted into bingo halls. Six of them have received listing orders. Tooting was the first to be listed in 1972, followed by those at Walthamstow, Harrow, Kingston, Woolwich and, most recently, Shrewsbury. The demolition of the Bedford Granada was especially sad as this would have adapted well to make a good concert hall or theatre.

Publicity brochure published for the opening of the Granada, Woolwich, south-east London, 1937

The Hall of Mirrors

Entrance to the Hall of Mirrors

Café-Restaurant on the Foyer Balcony

A glimpse of Granada splendour

Interior pages from the publicity brochure
published for the opening of the Granada,
Woolwich, south-east London, 1937, showing
the entrance to the Hall of Mirrors and the Hall
of Mirrors (top), and the auditorium and the
Café-Restaurant on the Foyer Balcony (bottom)

15: German Influence on British Cinema Design

A glance through P. Morton Shand's book *Modern Theatres and Cinemas* of 1930 reveals how influential German cinemas of the 1920s were on English cinema designs of the following decade. The book was part of this process, as were articles and illustrations in the various architectural journals. Some architects even visited Germany, most notably Ernest Wamsley Lewis. Although many exhibitors during the 1930s still demanded cinemas designed in a classical style derived from American models, architects increasingly turned towards trends developed in Germany.

The first generation of purpose-built German cinemas, dating from 1911 were more domestic in feeling than their English counterparts, and did not rely on heavy classical decoration. In plan they tended to continue the typical opera-house form, with narrow balconies extending towards the screen into slips. The UFA Theater Lichtspiele, Dresden, was a good example, with a horseshoe auditorium plan, the walls lined with boxes at first-floor level, and a splayed proscenium. Surfaces were broken with plaster texturing and all classical allusions were avoided. Of great interest was Oskar Kaufmann's Cines, Berlin, of 1912. Here, the neo-classical monumentality of the exterior walls was diluted by the softer lines of

the baroque-inspired pavilion roof. In the auditorium, the centrally placed box at the back of the balcony had a hint of the eighteenth-century court theatre. An element of Kaufmann's Theater am Kurfürstendamm, Berlin, was indirectly influential in Britain, namely its rococo shelf-like structure over the proscenium (referred to by Shand as 'airy Maria-Theresan chinoiseries'); this same structure was simplified by Fritz Wilms at the Piccadilly cinema in Berlin (1925), re-appears in Wamsley Lewis's New Victoria in London, and is then copied by William Trent and others in their work for Gaumont in the 1930s.

Hugo Pál's Marmorhaus cinema (1913), which still exists on the Kurfürstendamm, was a precursor of how the mainstream of German cinema architecture developed after the First World War. From 1925 cinema design philosophy veered away from pseudo-historicism towards a style based on a restrained neo-classicism. The inspiration for the stalagmite lighting used in the New Victoria can be traced back to various Berlin cinemas, such as the Capitol (Hans Poelzig, 1925) and the Utrechter Strasse Mercedes-Palast (Fritz Wilms, 1926). The extreme fan-formation plan of the Atrium (Friedrich Lipp, 1927) could well have influenced the layout of the

UFA Universum, Berlin, 1928

UFA Universum, Berlin, 1928

Gaumont Palaces at Hammersmith and Lewisham in London; and the semi-circular proscenium of the Gaumont Palace, Wood Green, London, originated in the Titania-Palast (Ernst Schöffler, Carlo Schloenbach and Carl Jacobi, 1928), although here the opening is compressed at the ends to create an arc.

The complete break with classicism in German cinema design came with the Deli Deutsches Lichtspieltheater, Breslau, of 1927, and the Babylon, Berlin, 1928-9, both by Poelzig, and the UFA Universum, Berlin, by Erich Mendelsohn of 1928. The Deli had a convincing modern-movement street façade; the Babylon, an uncompromisingly modern and stark auditorium; and the Universum is an icon of Continental modernism. The Babylon was too severe for it ever to be copied in Britain, and the nearest we got to it was in 1934 with the original Curzon cinema in Mayfair, London, by Francis Lorne, an 'art' cinema where advanced taste would be accepted. The Universum is a fine example of functionalism; the horseshoe shape of the auditorium, reflected in the exterior form, was created out of a continuous circulation space and cloakroom facilities running round both sides of the 'horseshoe', necessary in the cold winter climate of north Germany — this pre-auditorium space took up around one third of the entire building. In the auditorium no ornamentation was allowed to distract the audience, and lighting coves in the ceiling focused the eye towards the screen — it was the first 'machine for viewing the movies'. The prow-like fin, which pin-pointed the entrance, was to become a prevailing design talisman on the exteriors of the best Odeons a few years later. In this respect the angle tower on the Titania-Palast was even more important, the converging forms contributing to the resultant architectural impact.

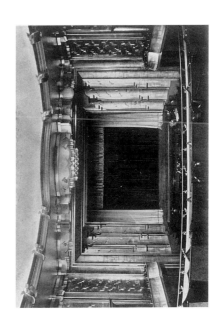

Atrium, Berlin, 1927

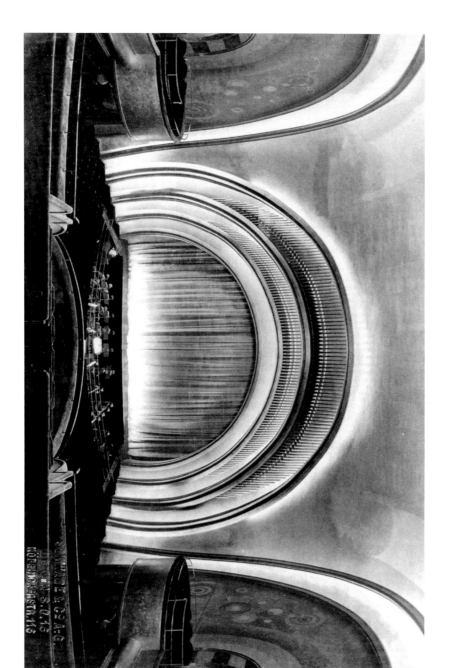

The exteriors of the Titania-Palast and the Lichtburg, Berlin, (Rudolph Fränkel, 1929) were built to demonstrate 'night architecture'. The fin tower of the Titania-Palast glowed with bands of light, and down-lighters from the cornice illuminated the flanking façades. The vertical strip windows of the Lichtburg were back-lit at night to define the form of the building, while searchlights scanned the blackened sky in a symbolic celebration of light. These innovations made a virtue of the self-advertising nature of the cinema; the German architects recognised that lettering and display should form an integral part of the design, not just appear as an after-thought.

Many of these cinemas did not survive the Second World War. The Universum still stands in the Kurfürstendamm, but the auditorium was wrecked when the building was converted into a multi-stage theatre; the Babylon can be found north of the historic centre of Berlin and the Titania-Palast remains in part a cinema, although the original auditorium has been floored-in for shops.

Titania-Palast, Berlin, 1928 (above and below)

16: Radical Changes in Cinema Architecture

We have seen how in the late 1920s some architects were searching for new expression that was neither classically inspired nor grounded in some exotic foreign origin. Robert Atkinson pioneered the trend with his simple façade for the Cameo, Charing Cross Road, London, in 1926, and his disciples, Leathart and Granger, had continued it with the Twickenham and Sheen cinemas.

An innovative auditorium could be seen at the Welwyn dual-purpose cinema/theatre at Welwyn Garden City, Hertfordshire, which opened in January 1928. The street front was designed to conform with the neo-Georgian style adopted by the architects Louis de Soissons and Arthur Kenyon for the civic and commercial centre of the new satellite city. But internally there was no such convention to observe, and decoratively the scheme looked to Germany. In the auditorium there was a hint of Oskar Kaufmann's rococo in the canopies above the wall niches. Each niche was filled with plate-glass acoustic reflectors rising the full height of the wall.

The big breakthrough came with the construction of the New Victoria in 1928-30. The architect, Ernest Wamsley Lewis, had studied in Germany and the USA in the late 1920s, the experience of which was reflected in the design of this most important cinema.

The New Victoria was a turning point in the development of the building type. While it was not slavishly copied, it did demonstrate to exhibitors and architects the possibilities of radically reinterpreting the image of the cinema building. Here was a festive alternative to ponderous classicism or neurotic whimsy, without the austerity associated with true modernism, as in the Babylon, Berlin, which was unsuited to entertainment buildings. For a full description of the New Victoria and Wamsley Lewis's involvement, see page 84. The influence of Wamsley Lewis's New Victoria was no more strongly felt than in the cinemas designed for Gaumont-British by William Edward Trent and his team of architects during the following decade.

The New Victoria Cinema, London 1930

Architect: Ernest Wamsley Lewis

The New Victoria, completed in 1930, represents a turning point in the development of cinema design. It demonstrated to exhibitors and their architects the possibilities of radically reinterpreting the image of the cinema. The revolutionary design introduced modernism to Britain in a popular form.

Ernest Wamsley Lewis, the architect of the New Victoria, was born in 1898. Wamsley Lewis served in the First World War, and then attended the Architectural Association school from 1920-5 under Robert Atkinson, after which he entered the offices of Collcutt and Hamp and then H. S. Goodhart-Rendel. In 1927 he won a travelling scholarship to study theatre design in America and Germany. On his return he set up practice and was engaged in 1928 by William Evans, the managing director of Provincial Cinematograph Theatres, to be the architect of the New Victoria. The site had been extremely expensive – £250,000 – and for the scheme to be viable the maximum number of seats had to be accommodated. Other architects had been interviewed but Wamsley Lewis won the commission by proving that it was possible to fit in over 3000 seats. Preliminary drawings indicate that a two-balcony scheme was proposed but this was abandoned in favour of a single-balcony auditorium. Wamsley Lewis used every inch available in a complex plan, in which the stalls were taken down to the basement, the side gangways fitted under the flanking streets, and the foyers 'sandwiched' into the area above the stalls ceiling and below the huge balcony.

For every fine building an enlightened client is almost as important as a talented architect. Evans gave Wamsley Lewis a free hand when it came to the style of the cinema. Wamsley Lewis recalled in later years that he was relieved at not being expected to decorate the interior with the 'usual architectural tripe'. When asked by Evans what the theme would be, Wamsley Lewis had to think on his feet and replied 'a mermaid's palace'. From then on marine motifs were incorporated although Wamsley Lewis's main inspiration had been recently gathered in Germany, in particular the Grosses Schauspielhaus of 1919 by Hans Poelzig (under whom he studied), with its extraordinary plaster stalactites. He was also influenced by Berlin cinemas of the mid-1920s (see Chapter 15).

Expressionism served as a canvas for the ravishing internal effects. Pale tints, using a plastic textured paint, were applied to the interior surfaces. A translucent effect could then be achieved by the use of concealed coloured lights controlled by dimmer switches. Additional light was provided by a cascade of glazed stalactites around the dome, while fountains of glass stood in niches beside the stage.

A 'sea' of seats were upholstered in contrasting deep blue-grey with a wave pattern. The acoustician, Hope Bagenal, specified 40,000 miniature spheres for the interior of the dome. Newbury Trent, the brother of PCT staff architect, William Trent, made relief panels in green Lap – a mysterious French synthetic material.

At first the unconventional streamlimed treatment of the exterior walls raised suspicion; passing bus conductors referred to it as 'Sing-Sing'. The façades were based on German precedents, such as Erich Mendelsohn's linear department store fronts and his Universum cinema in Berlin. Wamsley Lewis might also have been aware of the façade of Atkinson's 1926 Cameo cinema in London, to which the New Victoria bears an uncanny resemblance.

The building aroused much interest during and after construction. Morton Shand included it as a stop press item in his 1930 publication *Modern Theatres and Cinemas*, and there was

Foyer of the New Victoria, London, 1930

much favourable coverage in the architectural press. Not everyone could be convinced, however; Sidney Bernstein seemed blind to the New Victoria's beautiful interior, condemning it with: 'People don't want this sort of thing: they want architecture with marble columns, gilt and mirrors. This won't pay.' Some exhibitors believed Bernstein and clung to classical columns throughout the 1930s, but others accepted that sound films had brought a new realism to the screen which should be reflected in the buildings for the movies.

Wamsley Lewis never worked for PCT or their successors, Gaumont-British, again – despite completing the job dramatically under budget. This may have been due to professional rivalry in his relationship with Trent. Neither did Lewis design another complete cinema again, preferring to live quietly in Weymouth, building thatched cottages. He died in 1977 after ensuring that he had personally signed every one of his archive of drawings* for the cinema.

The New Victoria still stands, although now used as a theatre. A full restoration would be possible and highly desirable.

* In the Royal Institute of British Architects Drawings Collection, London.

New Victoria, London, 1930

17: Gaumont-British: Movie Palaces for the Nation

The Gaumont-British Picture Corporation had its origins in the French Gaumont Company founded by Léon Gaumont, who established the British offshoot in 1898 with A.C. Bromhead and T.A. Welsh. The British and French Gaumont companies separated in 1922 and Bromhead took control in collaboration with the Ostrer brothers, merchant bankers. In order to acquire more cinemas in which to show films made by the Gaumont company, and also to gain greater 'booking power' when hiring films from other distributors, Gaumont started to acquire whole circuits in 1926, including Biocolor Picture Theatres and the four Davis Pavilion cinemas in London (which brought them the huge Pavilion, Shepherd's Bush). A year later, the name of the company was changed to the Gaumont-British Picture Corporation. In 1929 they made their most important purchase, Provincial Cinematograph Theatres, who had ninety-six properties, bringing Gaumont-British's total holding to 278 cinemas. With the acquisition of United Picture Theatres in 1930, Gaumont-British controlled some 300 cinemas, making it by far the largest chain of cinemas in Britain at the time.

The PCT building programme continued after the amalgamation with Gaumont-British, and PCT's architect William Trent took charge of the new company's design. New cinemas opened in Edinburgh (1929), Bradford and London (1930), all named New Victoria after the London cinema, which was the first of these projects to start, in 1928. This cinema was designed by Wamsley Lewis as an isolated project for PCT and he did not work for the company again. Trent designed the Edinburgh cinema himself but at Bradford, a local man was brought in, William Illingworth, to design very much in the PCT company's idiom. It was to be a very large project, with upper and lower balcony levels and seating for 3318 altogether.

The first cinema to take the Gaumont name, with the suffix 'Palace', appeared in central Birmingham in February 1931. The architect was William Benslyn, former assistant to Robert Atkinson. For the exterior of this Gaumont Palace, Benslyn took his cue from his mentor and reproduced the white 'proscenium' window front surrounded by contrasting dark brick of Atkinson's Regent, Brighton. His auditorium side-wall treatment seemed to distantly echo Wamsley Lewis's rising mushroom forms to house uplighters as used in the London New Victoria, but here they looked more like inverted trumpets. There was also the familiar PCT domed ceiling.

In 1931, William Trent was busying himself with mock Tudor at the Gaumont Palace, Salisbury, and the company had to call in help from other practices, namely William Watkins of Bristol, whose office had been responsible for the PCT Regent in that city. Watkins designed four new Gaumont Palaces; at Coventry and Plymouth in 1931; and at Exeter and Barnstaple in the following year. Neither Watkins nor his chief assistant Percy Bartlett were as influenced by the New Victoria and German cinema architecture as Trent or Benslyn. The largest and most impressive of these four cinemas was the Coventry Gaumont Palace designed by Percy Bartlett, which repeated the elliptical proscenium of his Regent, Bristol. Although it did not feature the painted decoration of the Regent, it was enlivened by multiplying the number of mouldings and introducing cove lighting and, as ever, one of William Evans's beloved domes sailed overhead. This cinema was an exceptionally elaborate complex with two restaurants and a ballroom. The auditorium of the Gaumont Palace, Plymouth, was in a thoroughly art-deco style, likewise its scaled-down sister at Barnstaple. Exeter was of the stadium variety, reminiscent of the Regents at Dudley and Ipswich. PCT and Gaumont-British were the only circuit to build large cine-variety theatres on the stadium plan.

Benslyn produced a more successful version of his Birmingham cinema at Taunton in 1932, employing expensive cladding materials, such as the local Ham Hill stone used for the double-height architrave around the entrance and the first-floor balcony (a satisfying rationalisation of the Regent, Brighton, and Gaumont Palace, Birmingham, façades previously mentioned). Above the café windows, integral to this feature, the sculptural capabilities of the stone were exploited with a relief by Newbury Abbot Trent (William Trent's brother), described as symbolising 'Love and Life entangled by film'! The generous foyer was partly lined with Ancaster stone and travertine. Because the cinema was exposed on three sides, rather than hemmed in by other buildings, Benslyn was required to introduce features into the sea of bricks which make up the external face of any large auditorium. This he did by introducing aedicules with stepped tops, false buttresses, and smaller variations of the buttresses concealing ventilation extractors. The plaster decoration inside the auditorium carried the rising-mushroom forms to its conclusion, with stalactite electroliers cascading from the ceiling. An interesting planning device was that of the secondary entrance for the cheaper front-stalls seats at the stage end of the building, which seems somewhat like a return to the heavily segregated admission points of the Victorian theatre.

The Gaumont Palace, Taunton, still survives today as a bingo hall and is listed.

The company really got into its stride in 1932 with the opening of four Gaumont Palaces in the London suburbs of Peckham, Streatham, Hammersmith and Lewisham. Peckham and Streatham were designed by the firms of Verity and Beverley, and Nicholas and Dixon-Spain respectively, and Hammersmith was originally a Davis scheme employing Robert Cromie. This building has a vast fan-shaped auditorium, seating 3560, the plan dictated by the awkward site on a gently curving corner. The heavy main façade, 190-feet wide, is similar in form, but not in style, to Friedrich Lipp's Atrium cinema in Berlin. In the auditorium Cromie amalgamated elements such as the side-wall treatment from the Davis, Croydon (discussed in chapter 10), and ceiling coves derived from Lipp's Capitol, Breslau, with which he would have been familiar through Morton Shand's book *Modern Theatres and Cinemas*. The building stands today as Labatt's Apollo, a music venue.

William Trent's street front for the Gaumont Palace, Lewisham, was obviously inspired by Wamsley Lewis's New Victoria; employing artificial stone with streamlined banding and dark vertical elements in counterpoint, it was an entirely successful composition. The bulk of the edifice stood behind shops, although towering side façades were revealed in the adjacent streets, which Trent articulated with aedicules as Benslyn had done at Taunton. The plan was a brilliant use of the fan formation, with the poor visibility seating in the far corners eradicated and replaced by waiting areas. The auditorium walls were treated as giant arcades with columns opening out into the mushroom formation, again taken from the New Victoria. Pendant lights were suspended within the arches and those either side of the proscenium also held statues made by Newbury Abbot Trent again, representing, as stated in the opening brochure, 'the senses of Sight and Sound awakened and stimulated by the Film'. The ceiling consisted of a series of broad plaster lighting coves. The colour scheme was in silver and blue with the stage curtain in graduated shades of orange – it must have looked stunning. Even the organ console had special housing in keeping with the overall design. There were no historical allusions and, while not in the same league as the New Victoria, the Lewisham Gaumont Palace was one of the first cinemas in a modernistic vein. The opening programme was a tribute to home-grown British talent; Jessie Matthews starring in a Gaumont-British picture, *The Midshipmaid*, the Gaumont newsreel and an interlude on a British-made Compton cinema organ. Regrettably, this south-east London wonder is now supplanted by a traffic intersection.

The Gaumont Palace at Wolverhampton (1932) had a striking

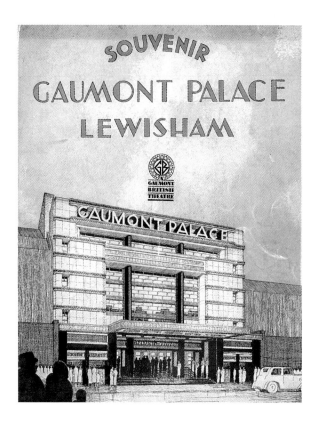

Programme for the Gaumont Palace,
Lewisham, south London, 1932

exterior situated on a corner, with horizontal banding as at
Lewisham, but using brick as the main facing material, rather than
artificial stone. At Cheltenham (1933) the banding was applied to
the auditorium walls and could well have been based on Gustav
Neustein's Stella-Palast in Berlin of 1929. The curved canopy above
the proscenium is derived from Wamsley Lewis's London New
Victoria. New Gaumont Palaces opened in 1934 at Doncaster
(where, in the auditorium, the horizontal banding was rather more
successfully handled and combined with lighting coves radiating
from above the proscenium as at Lewisham); Derby; Chelsea (with
an Oskar Kaufmann-inspired rococo ceiling); and Wood Green in
north London – the most remarkable of the group. At the latter no
dramatic architectural statement was possible in the narrow space
available between shops for the entrance façade (although Trent
was still borrowing from Wamsley Lewis in the design of the
doors), but in the auditorium he created a creditable crib of the
Titania-Palast in Berlin. Evans's favourite domed ceiling was finally
dead and instead we have streamlined mouldings turning in a vast

semi-circle above the proscenium, conceived as an arched rainbow
of light. There is rather more decorative plasterwork at Wood
Green than in the Titania-Palast, spoiling the purity of the original
concept. One difference between the latter and Wood Green was the
positioning of the organ pipes, which fill up the rainbow feature
in the Berlin example. A pictorial safety-iron, painted by Frank
Barnes, dramatically representing the signs of the Zodiac, could
be lowered into view. This could still be in position, although the
illustration may have been painted out. With the coming of wide-
screen films in the 1950s, the arched proscenium became a liability
and it was remodelled into a squarer form. Despite this alteration
there is still much to admire in what is now once again the Gaumont
Palace after a spell as an Odeon cinema. At the time of writing
the building is in use as a bingo hall, but it is likely to close during
the summer of 1996.

As previously mentioned, the Manchester Gaumont by Komisarjevsky, Benslyn and Morrison escaped from the Granada chain only
a short time before completion in 1935 and was, therefore, very

different to Trent's German-inspired style. From 1936, however, the German influence in Trent's work became less pronounced; the best of his output from this time was the Gaumont, Camden Town, London, of 1937. An unusual addition to the chain appeared a year earlier in 1936, in the form of a cinema at Chatham simply named the Palace. It was the work of Arthur W. Kenyon and while the exterior, entirely in brick, had a municipal air about it, the auditorium predicted post-war schemes, dispensing with a proscenium for a semi-circle of curtains dying into the splay walls. Just a few days before Christmas, 1937, George Coles's Gaumont State, Kilburn, in north-west London was opened. The largest cinema in England, with 4004 seats (only outstripped in seating capacity by the two gigantic Green's Playhouses in Scotland), this was the swan-song of the Gaumont circuit, although the scheme did not originate with the company and was stylistically very different from their other cinemas. For a full description of the Gaumont State, see page 90. The final Gaumont movie palace, at Holloway in north London, was the work of the American architect C. Howard Crane and opened in 1938. It could well have been designed at the same time as Crane was working on the Earls Court exhibition hall in 1937. It has one of the most powerful cinema exteriors ever built in Britain and had an excellent foyer, but the outdated and vulgar auditorium was destroyed in the Second World War, only to be rebuilt in a less extravagant form.

By the mid 1930s, Gaumont had realised that the future was less likely to be with huge multi-thousand seat houses than with cinemas in the 1500 capacity range. To this end they simultaneously developed a chain of more modest projects in quieter locations such as at Egremont, Wirral, in 1933, Stroud and Worcester (1935), Chippenham (1936), Carshalton and Finchley (1937), and Birkenhead and Dorking (1938). Both Egremont and Worcester were built on the stadium principle. Trent stayed in charge of design although local architects, like Harry Weston for Dorking and Carshalton, were introduced, Weston making a fine job of the latter with its heavily moulded auditorium ceiling.

To sum up the Gaumont contribution to cinema architecture, one has to regret that Wamsley Lewis was not further employed, but Trent did a good job in continuing his own sound work for PCT, grasping the need for a new style and finding it in both Lewis's genius and that of the German innovators of the previous decade.

Gaumont Palace, Wood Green, north London, 1934

Gaumont State, Kilburn, north London, 1937

Gaumont State, Kilburn, north
London, 1937

The Gaumont State, Kilburn, north London 1937
Architect: George Coles

The Gaumont State, Kilburn, in north-west London, with space for an audience of 4004, had the largest seating capacity of any cinema in England, before or since its construction. It was certainly the most ambitious project of both its architect, George Coles, and the promoters, the Hyams brothers.

Coles had designed the Trocadero, Elephant and Castle, for the same operators in 1930 and they wished to repeat the success of this cinema. Densely populated, Kilburn appeared to be a suitable location, and designing got underway in 1935 for what was intended to be named the Troxy cinema. Such were the complexities of construction on so enormous a building that it took over two years to complete, opening, with considerable publicity, including a special newsreel, four days before Christmas, 1937. By this time, the Hyams brothers, with their partner, Arthur Gale, had sold a majority holding of their company to the Gaumont-British Picture Corporation, hence the inclusion of 'Gaumont' in the name. The suffix 'State' may well originate in the fact that Coles's skyscraper-style tower over the entrance is reminiscent of New York's Empire State Building.

However, once inside, American modernity is abandoned in favour of a series of grand marble-lined Italianate foyers hung with chandeliers, leading to the classically inspired auditorium.

Coles made a convincing job of the former but the latter was, while still impressive, nowhere near as intoxicating as his Trocadero auditorium. The Hyams brothers obviously insisted on this reactionary classical theme but cost restrictions possibly also precluded another full-blown Trocadero-style treatment. The State was equipped with every movie-palace facility: a huge stage, a Wurlitzer which revolved whilst rising, a ballroom-cum-restaurant and a broadcasting studio in the tower for the resident orchestra.

Like the Empire in Leicester Square, filling the Gaumont State had become a problem by the late 1950s – some years back the late comedian Ted Ray recalled the impossibility of communicating with a sparse and scattered audience in so vast an auditorium. In 1959 the rear stalls were lost to what was one of the earliest conversions to the newly legalised bingo. The areas of the cinema devoted to this game gradually expanded, and today it is entirely a bingo hall, which has at least provided a use for this elephantine but amazing building.

18: The Odeon Style

What is the British perception of a cinema? So often the word Odeon springs to mind – it is almost a generic term. The Odeon group, chronologically the last of the great British cinema circuits to be created, was the most successful in imposing its identity on the nation's consciousness and maintaining a pre-eminent position to this day. This has been emphasised by the frequently changing ownership of Odeon's great rivals in the 1950s and 1960s, the former ABC chain, while since the take-over by milling magnate J. Arthur Rank in 1941, control of the Odeons has stayed constant.

The arrival of the mature Odeon style represents a sea-change in the thinking of what a cinema could be. Architecturally, there was a basic reversal of emphasis from interior to exterior. Gone were the elaborate interiors, be they classical or in some oriental fancy dress, and in their stead were clean-lined interiors with a minimum of decoration. The live elements, such as organs and ballrooms, were largely eradicated – the Odeon was not a leisure complex but purely a machine for viewing the movies. But externally the story was very different. The Odeon was highly visible on the High Street; it advertised itself in a flamboyant manner. At last a 'cinema style' had arrived, in a fusion of a suitable entertainment architecture with popular heroic modernism – the latter a concept which appealed to the film industry's thinking about itself at the time.

Oscar Deutsch, the founder of the Odeon circuit, was the son of a Birmingham scrap-metal dealer. Deutsch was born in 1893 and attended the best local school, the King Edward Grammar. While still at school he developed a passion for film, so although at first he joined the family firm, he soon left it, in 1920, to go into film distribution. Shortly afterwards Deutsch was attracted to film exhibition and began acquiring cinemas in the West Midlands. He built his first cinema at Brierley Hill in 1928, followed by the original Odeon in 1930, at Perry Barr, a northern suburb of Birmingham. It had a white rendered façade with Moorish overtones (the 'Odeon style' had yet to be invented), with the auditorium decorated in the same theme. As with the first Granada at Dover, the Odeon name had its genesis in somebody's holiday. Deutsch had deliberated for weeks trying to think of something original, when one of his partners in the business, Mel Mindelsohn, who had recently returned from a trip to Greece, came up with 'Odeion', the Greek name for the ancient amphitheatres. This was adopted in Anglicised form; it seemed especially appropriate as the first two letters matched

Deutsch's initials, and eventually the name became the basis of a slogan – 'Oscar Deutsch Entertains Our Nation'.

Deutsch's early Odeons were nearly all in the south of England. The Odeon at Weymouth, which opened in 1933 was a conversion of a bus garage. The Tolworth Odeon, built in advance of suburban development, opened in 1934, surrounded by fields. It was in the eight Odeons constructed between September 1933 and October 1935 in the new suburbs of outer London, designed by A. P. Starkey and his assistant, Frederick Adkins, that an architectural identity emerged. Where the site had sufficient width, Starkey and Adkins developed an unusual plan placing a single-storey foyer between higher symmetrical wings, accommodating shops and offices (for extra revenue), with the auditorium behind. The re-entry angles in the wings were enlivened with small lower blocks and a satisfying composition was achieved. The mould was cast at South Harrow, continued at Kingsbury and Colindale and found full expression at North Finchley, with its curving streamlined windows. Internally, the architects went for the stadium-type auditorium, avoiding the expensive balcony main beam. They were economical cinemas to build, costing under £20,000 (other cinemas being built at the same time cost around £40-50,000).

This horizontality, part of the search for a cinema style, was soon embellished by a vertical accent, the most readily recognisable aspect of the Odeon exterior. This first manifested itself at Worthing in March 1934, a more ambitious scheme than its London predecessors incorporating a square five-storey tower, a café and a cinema organ. The cinema lay back from the sea-front and the idea was to attract attention with the tower, which would otherwise have no purpose. The architects were Whinney, Son and Austen Hall, who produced a strong composition, contrasting brick with faience on the tower and café. Internally, a pattern was set for future Odeons, with a wide, splayed auditorium and restrained decoration. This cinema achieved listed status but was later disgracefully de-listed and, in 1987, allowed to be demolished. The square tower theme continued at Warley, Birmingham, later in the same year, where Deutsch put money into the eponymous cinema there. The architect, Thomas Cecil Howitt, had specified a tall tower but after Deutsch had stepped in this was reduced to a squat feature with an oversailing flat roof. Howitt adapted this feature for subsequent Odeons he designed at Weston-super-Mare, Bridgwater and Clacton. The Warley had originally been promoted by one W. H. Onions, who was also involved in a project for a cinema called the Beacon, at Kingstanding, another new area of Birmingham. To design the Beacon, Onions hired Harry Weedon, a prominent Birmingham architect who had recently built a factory for the Deutsch family.

The job was given to Weedon's chief assistant, Cecil Clavering, who developed a design incorporating faience-clad fins as a vertical feature on the main façade. His inspiration came from Julian Leathart's new Dreamland cinema, Margate, which had been widely published in the architectural press while still under construction in 1934 (see page 93). At Kingstanding, Clavering multiplied the fins into a group of three, but with the name of the cinema arranged horizontally lower down over the entrance doors, and only the sides of the fin feature were used for advertising, to carry the word 'Cinema' (at Margate, Leathart repeated the name 'Dreamland'). The original intention was for a searchlight to be mounted on the fins which would scan the night sky, like at the Lichtburg in Berlin. This idea was dropped when Deutsch took over the Beacon shortly before it opened in July 1935, renaming it the Odeon.

Deutsch was enormously impressed by the Beacon and engaged Weedon to mastermind the construction of all his new cinemas in towns north of Birmingham and in Wales. Cecil Clavering was to design three superb Odeons at Scarborough, Sutton Coldfield and Colwyn Bay, all opening within a few weeks of each other in 1936. They were the culmination of the developed Odeon house-style exterior, combining faience and high-quality facing brick. All three had corner sites where the positioning was exploited with rectangular and rounded elements converging in counterpoint. At Sutton Coldfield and Scarborough there were slab-edged fins, but at Colwyn Bay Clavering may well have derived the more three-dimensional fin from the Titania-Palast in Berlin. Shops, with flats above, were included here to maximise the commercial potential of the site. Scarborough and Sutton Coldfield still survive although the former, which had the most interesting auditorium, lost this interior recently despite listed status.

Clavering decided to take up an appointment in the Civil Service, and was replaced by Robert Bullivant. However, because the workload became so heavy, some five more architects were taken into Weedon's office – the staff complement is said to have grown from six to 140 within eighteen months. Harry Weedon held only an executive position and (with Andrew Mather in London), controlled the Odeon 'house style'. At Chester (1936) and York (1937), Bullivant produced schemes similar to those of Clavering, but designed to fall within the constraints of building in a historic city. Both cities banned faience, dictating brick as the facing material. They also stipulated that the squared-off standard Odeon lettering (invented by Pearce Signs) could not be used, and a serifed face had to be substituted. The nearest thing to an Odeon built in an historicist manner was at Faversham (1936), by Andrew Mather, where

92

Dreamland cinema, Margate, Kent
1935

Architects: Julian Leathart and
W. F. Granger

In 1931, the Dreamland amusement park in Margate was largely destroyed by fire, including the original cinema on the site, which was a conversion of an old music hall.

When the owners decided to re-build the entire site, the commission for a new cinema was awarded to Leathart and Granger as a result of a family connection between the amusement park owners and Leathart and Granger's partner, J.B. Iles.

The fun-fair lay behind terraces of Victorian boarding houses with only a relatively narrow frontage to the sea-front, therefore some arresting feature was required to attract the attention of holidaymakers as they cast their eyes along the promenade in search of entertainment. Leathart's audacious, soaring fin tower featuring the name 'Dreamland' served the purpose and may well have been inspired by the use of vertical lettering which had begun to appear on cinemas, particularly in the USA. A prototype of the fin tower could be found in Martin Punitzer's Roxy-Palast, Berlin, of 1929, and this would go on to become the predominant feature of many Odeon façades after Cecil Clavering successfully adapted the idea for the Odeon, Kingstanding, Birmingham, 1935.

The Dreamland elevation was also required to carry film publicity and, in Leathart's words, it 'represents an attempt to reconcile the necessity for large areas of advertising display on the main façade facing the sea, with the preservation of some architectural character and dignity. The design may be termed a background for predetermined publicity.'

The auditorium was, like those of the Odeons, relatively plain, although there were wall paintings in the foyer and café by Walpole Champneys.

The Dreamland cinema opened in March 1935, and was the last cinema to be designed by Leathart and Granger.

Dreamland, Margate, Kent, 1935

94

Odeon, Kingstanding, Birmingham, 1935

Odeon, Colwyn Bay, Clwyd, north Wales, 1936

The Odeon, Chingford, north London,
1935

Odeon, Muswell Hill, north London,
1936

Odeon, Well Hall, Eltham, south London,
1936

it had to fit in with numerous historic buildings. Some of the finest
Odeons by Weedon's collaborators were at Crewe, Leicester, Exeter,
Blackpool, Burnley, Chorley, Morecambe, Lancaster, Wolverhampton, Bradford, Rhyl and Newport (Gwent) – all good examples
of the house style. Morecambe and Blackpool, both by W. Calder
Robson, stand out from the others; the Odeon, Morecambe had a
strange glazed passage at third-floor level which was accentuated as
a point of interest for the main corner façade, while the Blackpool
Odeon was the largest Odeon ever built, with over 3000 seats.

Mather came to design most of the Odeons in the south of
England, along with George Coles. Generally, Mather's output was
less exciting that that of Weedon or Coles, with the exception of two
cinemas in the outer London suburbs, at Chingford (1935) and Well
Hall, Eltham, which opened a year later. Chingford, now demolished, had a magnificent tower in reconstructed stone, with stylised
figures near the summit supporting the central channelled section.
Well Hall survives, although in other hands, with its striking glazed
stair tower. Mather did, however, take on a talented assistant, Keith
Roberts, who produced some startling modern designs at the end
of the decade. The best of these was the large, uncompromisingly
modern Odeon at Camberwell in south London (1939), regrettably
recently demolished. It had huge areas of unrelieved brickwork
and was probably the closest the Odeons came to the 'International
Modern' style of the 1930s.

But the greatest architectural contribution in the London area
came from the amazingly versatile George Coles, who put aside
his grand classical interiors and Egyptian and Chinese fantasies
to create effective 'modernistic' or art-deco cinemas. Best amongst
them were at Isleworth (1935), Muswell Hill (1936), and Woolwich
(1937), which are all still with us today. Isleworth, regrettably
gutted internally, has an extraordinary, squat round-ended tower
which housed the outer lobby, while Woolwich has a faience façade,
extended to disguise the auditorium and encompassing a small car
park, which terminates in a kind of elongated finial. At night, neon
outlined the building in the true style of 'night architecture'. Externally, the Muswell Hill Odeon had to behave quietly, due to
objections raised by the church authorities opposite, but inside
Coles created one of his most effective schemes. A superb double-
height foyer, designed like a set from *Things to Come*, leads through
rotundas at ground- and first-floor levels to the auditorium, where
a lighting sconce plunges headlong from the back wall to the proscenium. The Odeon, Muswell Hill, now listed, was sensitively
'tripled' in 1974 and is still run by the Rank Organisation. By the
mid-1990s the interior looked sad and in need of redecoration. It
would be splendid if Rank would consider restoring it as the finest

remaining art-deco cinema interior in Britain. Coles completed two
other excellent projects in 1937, at Bury St Edmunds (a striking
façade with a streamlined central fin) and Bournemouth, with a
panelled and coffered auditorium.

After the opening of the rebuilt Empire in 1928, Leicester Square
was confirmed as the centre of London's cinema life, and Deutsch
decided to build a London 'flagship'. The only way he would be
able to get into the square would be to buy up a Victorian theatre,
demolish it and build on the site. The Alhambra, on the east side,
had been ailing for some time and was an easy quarry. See page 106
for a detailed description of the building of the Odeon, Leicester
Square.

In the nine years up to the Second World War, Deutsch opened
142 Odeons. The pace was frenetic, sometimes with as many as six
new cinemas opening in one month. To finance this prodigious
building programme, Deutsch established a complex finance
system, involving loans from the Eagle Star insurance company
paid directly to contractors, avoiding outlay himself. The insurance
company effectively owned the cinemas and Deutsch took the
profits less interest – a brilliant scheme. He also raised money
locally and every Odeon was a separate company, which dissipated
liability. All the seating, carpets and curtains were standardised and
there was even a technical manual to help architects lay out the
projection box, position admission points and advise on wall
finishes.

To further strengthen his position with film distributors, Deutsch
acquired around 130 cinemas during the same period from other
circuits. Most of them came from a combination of London and
Southern Super Cinemas, the Singleton circuit in Scotland,
Paramount and County Cinemas.

Following the launch of Paramount's two London première
cinemas, the Plaza and Carlton, in 1926-7, the company embarked
on a scheme to construct a small chain of large, luxury cinemas
designed primarily to preview their films in major British provincial cities. They retained the firm of Verity and Beverley, though
Frank Verity had retired (he died in 1937) and the practice was run
by his son-in-law and partner, Samuel Beverley. The first to see the
light of day was the Paramount, Manchester, opening in 1930.
Not surprisingly, there was a strong transatlantic influence in this
cinema; it was the only British cinema to have an American-style
mezzanine balcony inserted between the stalls level and the main
balcony. This tier was recessed below and behind the front of the
main balcony so as not to cut the top off the sight-lines from the
rear-stalls seats, a practice common in the largest movie palaces
in the USA. No space could be squandered in this expensive city-

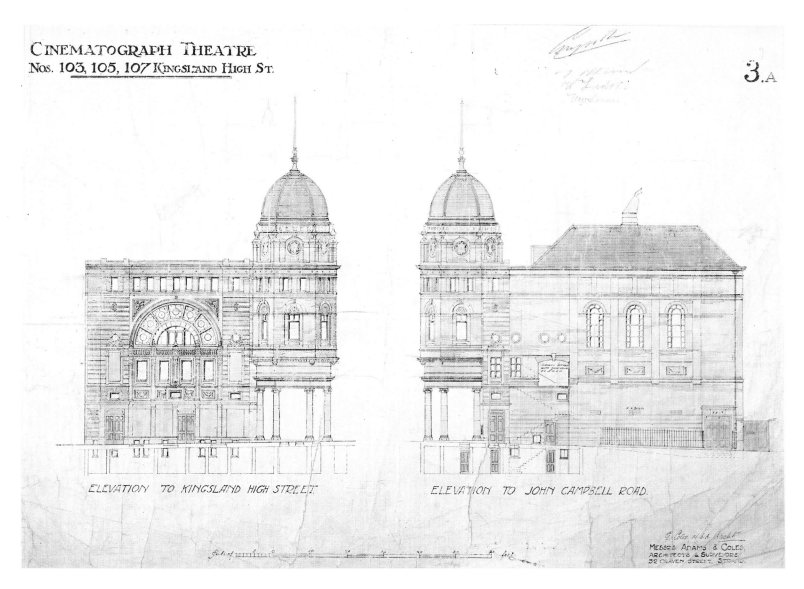

CINEMATOGRAPH THEATRE
NOS. 103, 105, 107 KINGSLAND HIGH ST.

3.A

ELEVATION TO KINGSLAND HIGH STREET.

ELEVATION TO JOHN CAMPBELL ROAD.

MESSRS ADAMS & COLES,
ARCHITECTS & SURVEYORS
32 CRAVEN STREET, STRAND

A contract drawing by the architect
George Coles for the Kingsland
Empire, Dalston, east London, 1915

Robert Atkinson's design, c.1920,
for the auditorium of the Regent,
Brighton, East Sussex

Carlton, Upton Park, east London
1928

Empire, Mile End, east London, 1939

Astoria, Finsbury Park, north London, 1930

Foyer of the Granada, Tooting, south London, 1931

Design by John Alexander for the
interior of the Northwick, Worcester,
1938

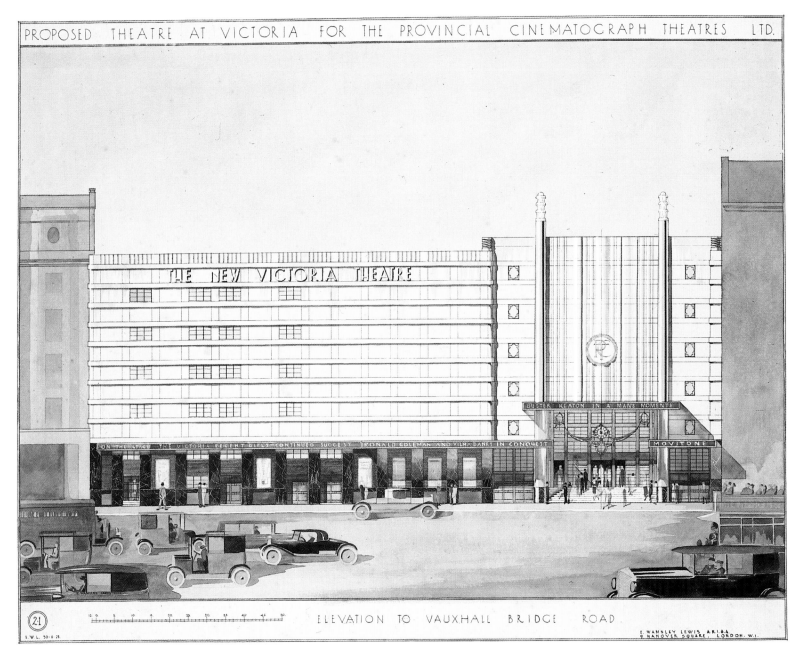

THE NEW VICTORIA THEATRE

BUSTER KEATON IN A MAN'S MOMENTS

ON THE STAGE THE VICTORIA REGENT GIRLS—CONTINUED SUCCESS   RONALD COLEMAN AND VILMA BANKY IN CONQUEST   MOVITONE

ELEVATION TO VAUXHALL BRIDGE ROAD.

E. WAMSLEY LEWIS A.R.I.B.A.
9 HANOVER SQUARE, LONDON. W.I.

Design of 1928 by Ernest Wamsley
Lewis for the New Victoria, London,
showing the cinema almost as built

Preliminary design of 1965 by Ernö
Goldfinger for the Odeon, Elephant
& Castle, south London

Harbour Lights cinema, Southampton,
Hampshire, 1995

Studios 1 & 2, Oxford Street (originally
built as the Cinema House, 1910),
London, showing the neon display
added in 1952

Odeon, Leicester Square, London,
1937

The Odeon, Leicester Square, London 1937

Architects: Harry Weedon, Andrew Mather and Thomas Braddock

Like the nearby Empire, the Odeon replaced a Victorian theatre, the Alhambra, which was demolished in November 1936. The Odeon opened barely a year later, indicating a feverish rate of construction.

For Oscar Deutsch's London flagship, the circuit's supervising architect, Harry Weedon, joined forces with one of the London area designers, Andrew Mather, to produce the scheme. After much deliberation, the architects came up with a façade of black polished granite, including a tower to carry the name of the cinema and a huge area for film advertising (a scheme said to be mainly the work of Thomas Braddock, one of Mather's assistants). This reversed the established Odeon house style of a light coloured front, and pursued the German principle of 'night architecture' (see Chapter 15), with the building outlined in brilliant neon after dark. The many surviving sketches* bear witness to the agonising that must have taken place over the appearance of the company's most important cinema. Existing structures hemmed in the site, except at the rear, where a ten-storey office building was built to provide additional revenue and to mask the stage house.

A rather dull foyer led to a sensational art-deco auditorium of ribbed fibrous plaster, which also aided the acoustics. The lighting within each cove operated in sequence, from above the proscenium to the back of the auditorium and then in reverse order when the lights went down. The splay walls carried low relief figures, the work of Raymond Britton Reviere, leaping towards the screen. The organ (the only five keyboard instrument installed in a British cinema) had a console specially designed to harmonise with the interior, and the seats were covered with fake leopard skin.

In 1967, when art deco appeared passé to all but those with the most advanced taste, this wonderful decoration was swept away to be replaced by acres of unrelieved blandness. Miraculously, the organ survived as did the safety curtain. Even the façade was unnecessarily tampered with. Today, the cinema remains the flagship of the circuit, the home of innumerable film premières. The idea of a stage show to accompany certain films has been revived in recent years but nothing can replace the loss of the magnificent art-deco interior, which would surely have become one of the tourist sights of London.

*In the Royal Institute of British Architects Drawings Collection, London.

centre site and therefore foyers were minimal. Even so, both the mezzanine and balcony were given separate approaches from the entrance lobby. The street elevations were rather disappointing, but the auditorium in Louis XV style was splendid. During the 1980s, however, it was subdivided into box-like mini cinema units. A recent idea to restore the auditorium is most welcome, and would provide a useful extra large performance space for Manchester.

The Newcastle Paramount came along a year later. Again, it had a severe street façade, although it did have an American-style vertical sign, rising almost the full height of the building. Inside, the expensive-to-construct mezzanine balcony was dispensed with, but luscious art deco was applied to the walls, attributable to Charles Fox, the American interior designer, rather than to Verity and Beverley. Indeed, the auditorium shows an uncanny resemblance to that of the Paramount in Aurora, Illinois, by the Rapp brothers, although this was completed in the following year. The side walls were broken up by a rhythm of pilasters which 'flowered' into glass lighting sconces programmed to change colour. The opening brochure describes the panels between the pilasters as being 'of silk, painted with figures suggesting Watteau'. A 'sequin-spangled net drapery' hung in front of the organ louvres 'which, moved by the current of air, scintillated with a remarkable effect …'. The stage presentations were advertised as coming 'direct from the Plaza Theatre, London' and included 'twenty-four Mangan Tillerettes' (Frank Mangan being the stage director at the Plaza). Most sensational were the French grey trouser suits worn by the usherettes. The Paramount cinemas brought American sophistication to the British provinces.

Two further Paramounts opened in Leeds and Liverpool, in 1932 and 1934 respectively. They were less elaborate but of comparative size to the other Paramounts, with just over 2500 seats. The Liverpool cinema was the first of the 'British style' Paramounts, having a longer, lower profile. The Leeds example, forming part of a new thoroughfare, the Headrow, had to comply with the predetermined appearance of the street, presided over by Sir Reginald Blomfield. Both cinemas are still open, but their interiors have now been altered out of recognition. Appropriately, the Paramount, Glasgow, opened on Hogmanay 1934. It had around 2800 seats and decoratively took its cue from the Atrium, Berlin, with the typical sculpted forms apparent in the ceiling. Two years later Paramount added another holding to their stock of cinemas in London, not this time designed as another West End preview house, but rather to serve a densely populated district of inner London which had hitherto been overlooked. Significantly, the entrance on a corner at the north end of Tottenham Court Road faced away from central

London. An Underground station nearby and the terminus of a trolleybus line ensured good communications. The interior was in a mature streamlined art-deco style similar to the work Verity and Beverley were producing for their other major client, Union Cinemas.

The final Paramount was built in central Birmingham. Opening in 1937, it had a sleek art-deco design which survived unscathed until the 1980s, even retaining the organ in regular public use. Oscar Deutsch's Odeon group acquired the Paramounts at Manchester, Newcastle and Leeds, together with the four London suburban Paramount-Astorias in November 1939. Subsequently four more went to Odeon leaving just the two West End première cinemas under Paramount's control.

County was a large chain of over fifty cinemas, which had been built up by an entrepreneur of Swiss origin named Charles John Donada. The majority of his properties had been acquired from other circuits, but County had also built some impressive cinemas. Among them were some of the better works by Robert Cromie, including the Regals at Wimbledon and Hull (1933 and 1934 respectively). At Wimbledon in south-west London, Cromie brought the 'proscenium' façade to its logical conclusion, surrounding two levels of windows above a banded ground-floor plinth by a sensitively proportioned area of faience, with the name of the cinema prominently displayed. The auditorium was entirely cove-lit and had acoustic channelling on the splay walls – it was one of the best resolved of his works. County's Ritz, Nottingham, by Verity and Beverley, had a highly successful art-deco auditorium, now long-since disappeared, lost when it became the first cinema to be twinned by Rank in 1965.

Oscar Deutsch died prematurely in 1941, and control of the Odeon circuit passed to J. Arthur Rank, bringing together exhibition and film production through his film studio at Pinewood. In 1948, Gaumont-British also fell under Rank's control, the combined chains creating a nationwide confederation of nearly 600 cinemas.

Paramount, Birmingham, 1937

The ABC circuit was the creation of a Scottish solicitor John Maxwell. Maxwell was born in the mid-1870s and had built up a solicitor's practice in Glasgow. Around 1908 he became aware of the commercial opportunities of film exhibition when handling the legal aspect of a cinema transaction. From 1912 he began acquiring cinemas and in eight years he was running twenty cinemas registered in the name of a company called Scottish Cinema and Variety Theatres. Soon after, he moved into film production and distribution in London purchasing Elstree studios as a base for his new company British International Pictures, who distributed their first talkie *Blackmail* in 1929. Associated British Cinemas began as the exhibition arm of BIP in 1928, by which time Maxwell had taken control of approximately forty-four cinemas.

The first new cinema building projects by the company were in Scotland; the Ritz, Edinburgh, in 1929, for which the architects were William Riddell Glen and Albert Gardner (from whom Glen had learnt about cinema design) and then, later in the same year, the larger Regal, Glasgow, by Charles McNair. Even grander was their next project, the Savoy, Dublin, also in 1929. The Savoy was a promotion of Savoy Cinemas, one of the companies Maxwell had acquired to create ABC. It was the largest the group was ever to build, with 2792 seats, and was also interesting for its 'atmospheric' auditorium by the interior designer W. E. Greenwood, his most successful essay in the genre. Savoy Cinemas were keen on very large schemes, but Maxwell's influence brought the average size down to well under 2000 seats for the company's major construction campaign of the 1930s. Savoy's architect, F. C. Mitchell, had started work on another huge cinema at Brighton but it was completed by William Glen after he was taken on as a permanent member of staff. Here, over 2500 seats were fitted into a cramped site in the oldest part of the Regency resort. There were two entrances; one facing into the town and the other on the sea-front to attract passing holidaymakers. Very unusual was the situation of a car park in the basement. The exterior was undistinguished but it had an attractive auditorium decorated in Japanese and Chinese motifs, now lost to later alterations.

In Birmingham, ABC acquired the Regent in New Street, formerly a Masonic Hall. Glen reconstructed the auditorium on three levels within the nineteenth-century retaining walls, and it opened as the Forum in 1930. This too has now been obliterated.

Ritz, Belfast, Northern Ireland, 1939

The auditorium was influenced by the fashion for atmospheric decoration with plaster cypress trees and vines draped around the balcony slips, and a 'sunburst' crowning the proscenium. Two excellent auditoria, which combined an art-deco ethos with a lingering atmospheric flavour, followed in the Forum at Liverpool (1931) and the Savoy at Wandsworth, London (1932). Both had wide overarching false prosceniums and tall niches in the splay walls. The Liverpool Forum had unique low-relief plaster panels representing skyscrapers, including the then brand new Chrysler building in New York. The cinema is now listed and although it has been subdivided, those panels survive to this day. The Wandsworth cinema was demolished in 1960.

During the high watermark of cinema construction in the years leading up to the Second World War, ABC completed some eighty new openings, with William Glen as the company architect in charge of design. In order to cope with this prodigious workload he must have had many assistants. It was a fine body of work, although it has tended to be overlooked in favour of the contemporary Odeons. This is possibly because Glen's exteriors were generally undemonstrative, not displaying the architectural fireworks that the Odeon architects were encouraged to indulge in. Glen came into his own, however, when designing the interiors of his cinemas. His planning and handling of interior volume had great fluency – he was particularly adept at foyers and some of them were of double- or even triple-height proportion, such as at Streatham in south London. Access to the stalls would be down wide steps in between symmetrical flights of stairs to the balcony. Glen's auditoria were cohesive; after the early examples, they stylistically settled down into what would then have been termed 'modern'; there were no Tudor, Gothic or Spanish ABCs and there were only a few, not very successful, returns to classicism. The seating capacity of the average ABC was somewhere around 1500 seats, and Maxwell's cinemas were more expensive than the Odeons, costing around £50,000. He was less enamoured of the 'machine for viewing films' principle than Oscar Deutsch but, nevertheless, there were not many frills. Shallow stages were sometimes provided, but rarely used, the variety aspect in the programme being dictated by the intensity of the local competition; restaurants were the exception not the rule; and only about a third of the cinemas included an organ, and these were nearly all of a relatively small standard design from the British maker Compton, cheaper than the original American Wurlitzer, although this deficiency was invariably compensated for by a gigantic illuminated console rising from the orchestra pit. Maxwell was of the opinion that people visited cinemas primarily to see the film and wished to find themselves in comfortable surroundings, warm in winter, cool in summer, and in a pleasing environment. Not being heroic interiors there were few mourners at their passing, which makes those that do survive all the more important.

The following are worthy of mention: the Regal, Hammersmith, west London, where plaster galleons set sail on the ante-proscenium walls (mutilated); the Ritz, Muswell Hill, north London (demolished); the Savoy, Stoke Newington, with a passable façade and superb auditorium (ground level altered); the Savoy, Northampton, with the same qualities (listed, although closed as a cinema in 1995); the Regal, Ilford, with a wonderful streamlined ceiling (converted into nightclub); the Empire, Mile End, east London, with an auditorium reminiscent of Trent's German-influenced Gaumonts (survives although closed); the Royal, Plymouth, a diluted version of the same type (split between bingo and cinema); the Regal, Streatham, south London, for its magnificent foyer (open as a Cannon cinema) and the Regal, Old Kent Road, London, with an Odeonesque exterior (demolished).

In 1937 ABC acquired Union Cinemas, giving the company an extra 136 outlets. This came about through the financial collapse of the Union Company following the death of the chairman, David Bernhard, and John Maxwell wasted no time stepping in. Union had grown too rapidly in just a few years, sometimes acquiring all the cinemas in a town to prevent competition from other circuits. But the real financial problems were caused by overspending on large and lavish new cinemas, erected in quick succession and equipped with expensive fittings, such as chandeliers and Wurlitzer organs with unbelievably ornate glass console surrounds. Union regularly employed three architects: Samuel Beverley of Verity and Beverley, Leslie Kemp of Kemp and Tasker, and Robert Cromie.

Union had acquired three superior cinemas, all named Regal, and designed by Robert Cromie. They were at Beckenham (1930), Kingston-upon-Thames (1932) and Bexleyheath (1934). The Regal, Kingston, was the largest of this group, with almost 2500 seats. Predictably, the auditorium was very similar to Cromie's exactly contemporary Gaumont Palace, Hammersmith. The Regal survives today as a bingo hall and is listed. The Beckenham Regal also still stands, as a Cannon cinema, although the interior has been lost to subdivision.

Of the cinemas constructed by Union, it is worth highlighting two named Ritz by Cromie, at Ipswich and Chatham, both built in 1937, the former with an auditorium in streamlined panelling – the surfaces largely governed by acoustic considerations – and the latter, one of Union's largest projects, with 2322 seats. The Ritz, Hereford, was designed by Leslie Kemp. It was an isolated building with a blockish exterior intended to terminate in shops and a waiting room for the adjacent bus station, though this feature was never completed. Kemp built another interesting cinema for the company at Dunstable (1937) – actually named Union – and this still stands as a bingo hall. For the Ritz, Barnsley, Verity and Beverley produced a decoratively restrained but sizeable auditorium. Ritz and Regal were the two most popular names for the Unions, although occasionally they used the company name for the cinemas themselves, as at Dunstable and Luton. Regrettably, not more Union cinemas had real architectural distinction.

John Maxwell died in 1940 and after the War there were modest openings during the 1950s and 1960s. The 1970s saw the period of subdivision of auditoria into smaller units on a very ambitious scale, and more was destroyed of the interiors than in Rank's Odeons, who treated their cinemas with greater sensitivity. At its peak, ABC operated over 400 cinemas, the vast majority taken over from other operators. Despite the dark days of swingeing closures many have survived to be run by Cannon-MGM. At the time of writing, the ABC name is about to be reinstated on these old cinema façades.

Regal, Old Kent Road, south London, 1937

After the success of their vast Playhouse cinema in Glasgow, the exhibitors, George Green Ltd, wished to build on a similar scale elsewhere. For their second opus, in 1936, they chose Dundee. Their architect, John Fairweather, once again lined the auditorium (which held 4114) with massive Corinthian columns. Two levels of private boxes filled the spaces between the two bays closest to the stage. The foyer block and cinema restaurant were designed by the distinguished modernist architect, Joseph Emberton. The upper section of Emberton's street front took the form of a vertical fin to advertise the name of the cinema – rising up in the sheer white render of international modernism. The bulk of this important cinema was lost in a fire in August 1995 but the tower survives. George Green Ltd also built other large Playhouse cinemas at Wishaw in Lanarkshire and Ayr on the Clyde coast. Exhibitors of a different hue, the Black family, opened the huge Regal, Sunderland in 1932. It had a narrow entrance beneath a tower, but inside the space widened out to create exceptionally generous foyers.

The Odeon house style became highly influential and other operators would request similar designs. The Regal, Old Kent Road, London, by William Glen, built for ABC, had an Odeon-inspired tower with fins, and these same components can be found in the work of the Nottingham architect, Reginald Cooper. Most of Cooper's cinemas were on his home territory and were medium-scale super cinemas built to seat around 1000 people. The Metropole, Sherwood (1937), and the Ritz, Ilkeston (1938), had well-composed façades incorporating slender fins. The Adelphi, Bulwell, also from 1938, had a fine rotunda tower and the Roxy, Daybrook, of a year earlier, had a slab tower relieved by horizontal banding. Cooper's interiors were reminiscent of Robert Cromie's work; the heavily sculpted auditorium of the Savoy, Lenton Abbey was particularly successful. It survives as a cinema with two small auditoria under the original balcony. Cooper is on record as insisting on specifying every inch of the interiors himself rather than handing them over to a consultant designer or a fibrous plaster manufacturer. The Ritz, Ilkeston is now a bingo hall, as are the Adelphi, Bulwell, and the listed Capitol, Radford, the latter with an entrance inspired by Mendelsohn's Universum in Berlin.

A similar Odeon influence was present in the work for independent exhibitors by Leslie Kemp, as could be seen in his exotically named Havana cinema, Romford, of 1936. It had a distinctive

114

Green's Playhouse, Dundee, Scotland,
1936

advertising slab tower, this time in black faience. In Scotland,
T. Bowhill Gibson designed one of the best Odeon-inspired cinemas,
the County, Portobello, Edinburgh (1939), which included a glazed
fin, back-lit, with a colour change mechanism.

Other architects were striving to produce something more
unconventional. Viewed from today's perspective as typical art
deco, E. Norman Bailey's Regal, Uxbridge (1931), had a vaguely
Egyptian-flavour street façade, with the name of the cinema picked
out in coloured faience. The exterior was no preparation, however,
for the auditorium, where the ceiling was a riot of fibrous plaster
mouldings, scallops and swirls, and the cove-lit proscenium had a
unique curvaceous form, presaging the shape of the early television
screen. The Regal, although listed, is now cluttered with the para-
phernalia of a nightclub, completely alien to the spirit of this
wonderful art-deco interior. A like fate has befallen the once ravishing streamlined auditorium of the former Grosvenor cinema,
Rayners Lane, Harrow (1936), by Frederick Bromige, but at least
here the street front has been restored. Well sited, almost opposite
the Underground station, the main point of interest is the so-called
'elephant's trunk', which plunges from the parapet to the top of the
rounded canopy, ostensibly to support the revolving structure which
carries the fattened-up lettering of the cinema's name. To either
side are areas of glass, lighting the stairs up to the balcony. Behind
the entrance doors was once a delightful sunken café, the epitomy
of art-deco elegance. Bromige designed few cinemas, but those he
did ensured his name as a intriguing architectural 'rogue' if ever
there was one. He built three more in the west-London suburbs,
all promoted by an independent company but later sold to major
chains. For his extraordinary façades he favoured white painted
cement render which could be more easily moulded to his bulbous
forms than the more expensive faience. The double-curved front of
the Dominion, Southall (1935), breaking forward with a prow-like
fin, looked like gigantic book-ends with the books missing. The
equally dramatic front on the Harrow Dominion (1936) bulged
menacingly until ABC, no doubt unwilling to continue coping with
the prodigious maintenance problem of such a façade, re-clad it
with metal sheeting in the 1960s. At the Acton Dominion, large
areas of brick counted against achieving such a dramatic effect.
Curiously, the huge window above the entrance is actually
supported by the canopy.

Another architect in broadly the same category was Henry Elder
of Manchester, whose first cinema, the Rota, Denton of 1934, was
built for a small local circuit, Jackson and Newport. The foyer block
here was in the form of a drum, with wide overhanging eaves and
a canopy. The spherical theme continued in the auditorium, where

Regal, Uxbridge, west London, 1931

Grosvenor, Rayners Lane, Harrow, west
London, 1936

strong downward curves in the side-wall treatment dictated the
form of the proscenium and a cove-lighting trough in the ceiling.
Elder's most radical scheme, the Longford at Stretford, east of the
city centre, appeared in 1936. The main front, entirely faience-clad,
was set back behind a forecourt. This façade curved in at the top
and is said to represent an old-fashioned cash-register. The subsidiary elevation in a side road features an obelisk above a circular
canopy, set in front of an elliptical tiled wall. This implied phallic
motif and the main front, symbolise Elder's concept of cinema as
a marriage of sex and commerce. The County, Reddish, had a more
restrained brick exterior, but the proscenium broke new ground by
dispensing with stage curtains and introducing a screen intended to
'float' on a blue background. At the outbreak of the Second World
War, Elder was working on a revolutionary project for a vast 2000-
seat egg-shaped cinema to be built in Manchester. It was to have
been constructed in reinforced concrete with the screen in the
pointed end of the egg, which would have had to be supported on
stilts. The war killed the scheme and Elder eventually emigrated
to Canada.

115

David Evelyn Nye was certainly no 'rogue' architect, his carefully
designed schemes often having to fit into a sensitive local environment. As a newly qualified architect, Nye entered the field in 1936
with the Embassy, Maldon, for Shipman and King, a circuit which
specialised in building medium-sized cinemas for middle-class
communities in the south of England. The Embassy's façade and
auditorium were somewhat bland, but the zebra-striped café, the
work of interior designers Mollo and Egan, was sensational. Nye
improved in the following year, creating another Embassy (the
chosen name of many of Shipman and King's cinemas) at Esher,
an expensive Surrey suburb. The outside had to be neo-Georgian
but within, fibrous plaster openwork panels and stencilling suggested tropical vegetation, with light diffused through a pergola
in the ceiling. The front-stalls floor has a 'reverse rake', causing the
seats in that area to incline slightly backwards. Articles in architectural journals at the time proposed that by using this technique,
sight-lines would be improved. Nye may well have been familiar
with this theory but when questioned in later life about the feature,
he provided no learned thoughts, simply explaining that it saved
on excavation costs, the cinema being built into a hillside. The
Embassy auditorium can still be seen today almost unaltered.
The Rex, Berkhamsted (1938), had a modernistic exterior and
one of Nye's most effective auditoria, decorated with shell motifs.

Also of note, is the Embassy, Peterborough, built by Nye for the
Bancroft family in 1937 and originally planned for both film and
live performances. It served both purposes for the first sixteen years

of its existence, until films took over permanently in 1965. In an ingenious 'v'-shaped plan (the building was situated at the junction of two streets), the auditorium occupied the wider end, with the stage-house and six storeys of dressing rooms crammed into the apex. A series of string-courses relieved the otherwise blank exterior walls and, in theatre fashion, the fine art-deco auditorium (now gutted) featured a balcony built in close proximity to the proscenium, but side boxes were avoided. The Embassy at Esher and the Rex at Berkhamsted are both listed; the former currently still shows films but the Berkhamsted cinema has been derelict for some time pending redevelopment or restoration.

Sidney Colwyn Foulkes received his architectural training at the highly regarded Liverpool School of Architecture. Foulkes's best-known work, the Palace cinema, Conway, appeared in 1936. The exterior walls reused stone from a house previously on the site to conform with the historic surroundings. The interior did not have to follow the same precept and Foulkes produced a simple but elegant auditorium. Columns flanking the proscenium supported a curving architrave decorated with film stars' heads in relief. Above, coloured lighting effects were projected onto a semi-dome from emplacements in the balcony front. The stage curtains were also bathed in colour from footlights and overhead battens. Publicity at the time claimed that 'the lighting has four hundred tints and every imaginable combination of colours can be displayed by an electrical apparatus that maintains continually changing colour symphonies' – one dial in the projection room activated the whole operation. Lighting systems were seen by architects and exhibitors as an alternative way of creating an up-to-date interior without the expense of elaborate architectural effects. This important cinema can still be seen in Conway but listed status has so far proved elusive.

Foulkes repeated the same interior formula elsewhere but, like Henry Elder, his most interesting scheme remained unrealised. The Rex, Birkenhead, was to have had a free-standing proscenium positioned in front of a huge cyclorama merging in with the walls and ceiling of the auditorium. Elaborate colour lighting effects could then play onto the entire domed surface. The outbreak of war brought construction of the Rex to an end. The still extant Apollo, Ardwick, Manchester (1938), by Peter Cummings and A.M. Irvine, has a coffered and domed ceiling above the proscenium, incorporating a similar lighting system.

None of the bright young sparks of the modern movement in architecture seem to have gone in for cinema design. Perhaps their ideas were too avant-garde for exhibitors to contemplate employing them. The Royal Institute of British Architects Drawings Collection houses a series of drawings by members of the Tecton partnership,

Anthony Chitty and Godfrey Samuel with Valentine Harding. Chitty's drawings are for the 'Lyric Variety Theatre', Ipswich, and are dated December 1934. The scheme included a large two-level cinema with a stage, and a ballroom on the first floor, all set behind a forecourt of shops. The Samuel and Harding project of 1937 proposed a new front for the Hippodrome, Ilford, a theatre by Frank Matcham which was bombed in 1941 and subsequently demolished. The Ipswich proposals are particularly lively and one can only wish that both sets of drawings had become reality.

Rex, Berkhamsted, Hertfordshire, 1938

Café at the Embassy, Maldon, Essex, 1936

21: Cinema Interior Designers

But what of interior decorators, whose labours are often difficult to distinguish from those of the architect? Some architects desired and were given control of the interior, such as Julian Leathart, George Coles and Reginald Cooper. Others were happy to let an interior designer take over, and in some instances a designer was imposed by the exhibitor, such as at the Paramount, Newcastle, where Charles Fox from the USA introduced a transatlantic look to the interior of Verity and Beverley's shell. Most notable among cinema decorators was Theodore Komisarjevsky, who was given a free rein inside Sidney Bernstein's Granada cinemas.

A number of fibrous plaster decoration contractors became involved in designing, the most well known being the firm of Mollo and Egan, established by Eugene Mollo. The famous London furniture emporium, Maples, had a decorating department active in cinema work. Stencilled and air-brushed designs were much in evidence in the smaller super cinema of the late 1930s as an economical and effective way of enhancing the interior without resorting to costly heavy ornament. These charming painted schemes are now very rare. The dirt and staining caused by years of audiences smoking, necessitated cinemas being redecorated in the 1950s and 1960s, by which time the original designs looked passé and were obliterated.

An exponent of this type of decoration was Gerald Ososki, an employee of Eugene Mollo who went on to found Roffe Ltd in 1934. Ososki worked on cinemas for the Union and County circuits, including the Regals at Wimbledon and Hull and the Ritz, Huddersfield. The firm also patented 'Marb-l-cote', a surface material composed of marble and stone dust with mica, which could be applied to fibrous plaster creating a stippled effect in relief. Precious stencil painting still survives at the Tivoli, Wimborne Minster.

The name John Alexander will survive due to the remarkable legacy of his highly accomplished drawings for cinema interiors, many of which are now in the care of the Royal Institute of British Architects and the Victoria and Albert Museum. They include both refurbishment projects and new proposals, some of them exciting and innovative. The one surviving documented interior by Alexander is the Northwick, Worcester, of 1938 (see p.101). The plain brick exterior (by C. Edmund Wilford) houses an astonishing art-deco auditorium with mythological figures in fibrous plaster on the ante-proscenium splays. Complex stencilling also extends onto

the rear walls and ceiling. The plaster was repainted in totally inappropriate colours during the Northwick's days as a bingo hall, but
in 1993-4, under new management as a live music venue, English
Heritage have been allowed to research the correct colour-scheme
for the plaster and to restore the stencil designs.

Decoration underway on the niches
above the loges at the Granada,
Tooting, south London, 1931

Gerald Ososki with a colleague
standing before one of his stencilled
designs

22: The Newsreel Cinema

The newsreel cinema existed to fill a niche, that of news in pictures, which could not be adequately exploited by newspapers. The coming of sound had enormously increased the effectiveness of newsreels, hence whole programmes, lasting about an hour, were devoted to news and documentary 'shorts', sweetened by the new animated cartoons – *Silly Symphonies* – emerging from the Walt Disney Studio. Newsreels were unsatisfactory, however, in their lack of immediacy; they were generally only able to record pre-planned events such as sporting events, state occasions and the arrival in Britain of the latest Hollywood film star. Before the arrival of television it was quite acceptable to hear a news story on the 'wireless', read it the next day in a newspaper and then see it again up to a week later at a cinema. The 'haunted fish tank' in the corner of the sitting room removed the role of the newsreel cinema from life's agenda.

The newsreel cinema was born in New York in 1929, and the Gaumont-British Movietone News Theatre, a conversion of an existing cinema, opened on London's Shaftesbury Avenue a year later. It was an instant success and led to offshoots throughout the West End and in many provincial city centres. Two remarkable newsreel cinemas were built as a collaboration between Capital and Provincial News Theatres and the progressive Southern Railway, at Victoria and Waterloo stations in London, in 1933-4. Their architect was Alister Gladstone Macdonald, the son of Britain's first Labour Prime Minister, Ramsay Macdonald. Both cinemas were in extremely constricted locations, with compact auditoria well insulated against the noise of busy railway termini, where steam engines were still in evidence. The inviting façades faced into the stations, the intention being for passengers to while away time waiting for trains inside the cinema – today we shop for socks. At Victoria, Macdonald used a linear streamlined styling, whereas the Waterloo example was more Corbusian; the bulky auditoria were ingeniously hidden in the station structure. Because of the extreme shortage of space, the Waterloo news cinema had a unique film-presentation system, whereby the image was projected down a tunnel-like chute onto a glass screen. It was then reflected in an inclined mirror within the proscenium, which was effectively the cinema screen. The system must have been found wanting, for it was eventually replaced by conventional projection and a normal screen. Both these news cinemas have long since been demolished.

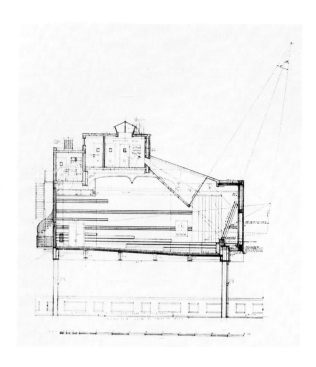

Section of the Waterloo Station
newsreel cinema, showing the film
projection system

Victoria Station newsreel cinema,
London, 1934

Robert Atkinson also contributed a news cinema, in another location where space was at a premium, Piccadilly Circus, on the same site where Birt Acres had set up his early film show in 1896. The Eros News Theatre (1934), a conversion of a café of the same name, managed to fit a small balcony into an auditorium which was higher than it was wide. A staircase balustrade depicted, in stylised form, a newsreel cameraman and his tripod camera. After the cinema closed in 1985 this delightful feature was rescued by the Museum of London. On the other side of the Circus, the basement Monseigneur News Theatre was created by Cecil Masey out of the restaurant of the same name, in just twenty-two days in the autumn of 1934. Part of it was a café, where you could view the newsreels and eat simultaneously. Because newsreel cinemas often had High Street locations, 'ladies only' seats were sometimes provided for exhausted 1930s housewives.

Following the demise of the newsreel, many of these cinemas found a new life showing pornographic films. Now that video has removed this market, the newsreel cinema has become part of cultural history. However, a provincial newsreel house remains in use as the Tyneside Film Theatre (formerly the News Theatre, designed by George Bell, 1937) in Newcastle, where the small auditorium has been very little altered.

23: Music for the Movies

The phrase 'music for the movies' may conjure up an image of a lone pianist churning out appropriate melodies for hours on end at an upright instrument under the screen, adapting the music to suit the mood of the movie – *allegretto* for a car chase, *pianissimo* for a love scene. But, in the silent days, the grander the picture palace, the more imposing the scale of musical accompaniment, with ten- and twenty-piece orchestras becoming common. With the arrival of the talkies, live musical accompaniment for films became a thing of the past – 'it's all in the can' was a catch-phrase of the time. At the largest establishments with a fully-equipped stage, where cine-variety was still an attraction, a pit orchestra would be on hand to accompany the acts. Then the era of the dance-band arrived, taking the musicians out of the pit and onto the stage. Sometimes a band would be booked to appear at two cinemas simultaneously; in London, the New Victoria and the Dominion often shared the same band, with a waiting coach to whisk them between their featured 'spots'.

If the cinema building had a voice, then it was that of the organ – this mighty instrument would roar up in front of the screen in a blaze of glitz and ballyhoo, only to sink back down as the footlights faded and the tableau curtains began to part. But why an organ in a cinema, what was its origin? Returning to the silent era, the management of the larger cinemas had to solve the problem of all-day adequate film accompaniment. The hours were long and a band could not play continuously. Short of duplicating the complete orchestra, some alternative instrument, more effective than a piano, was required. Organs started to be installed in cinemas before the First World War but these were not cinema organs as such, being basically church instruments.

The cinema organ proper was the invention of a former Liverpool telephone engineer, Robert Hope-Jones (1859-1914), and it represented the culmination of the romantic development in organ music during the nineteenth century. His invention consisted in modifying the church organ, to 'liberate' it by electrifying the complicated action connecting the console to the pipes. In the early 1900s Hope-Jones emigrated to the USA where he built a number of organs for churches, hotels and theatres, only to go bankrupt in 1910. The Rudolph Wurlitzer company, previously manufacturers of automatic musical instruments, stepped in and acquired the Hope-Jones company and its founder, realising the potential of exploiting the instrument for the cinema. Between 1911 and 1925 over 1000 'Wurlitzer Hope-Jones Unit Orchestras' (significantly not called organs) were constructed and installed in cinemas. The first one to cross the Atlantic was installed in Provincial Cinematograph Theatre's Picture House, Walsall, in 1925. Meanwhile, another English organ builder, John Compton, had been thinking along the same lines and had installed an instrument in the County cinema, Sutton, four years earlier. A second English maker, the traditional organ builder Hill, Norman and Beard, installed their first 'Christie' cinema organ (named after the owner of the firm, John Christie, of Glyndebourne fame) in 1926.

The 'liberation of the action' as described above, was obviously vital to cinema installations, as the console was sited in the orchestra pit and the pipes in their 'chamber' placed elsewhere. There was much controversy between organ builders and architects over the best location for the organ chamber, which could be in the side walls, under the stage or over the proscenium. The other great variance from the church organ was in tonality; the idea was for the organ to emulate the orchestra, for which during the silent days it was thought of as a substitute. To achieve this, the makers created the maximum tonal contrast in the instrument, employing lush, mellow stops such as the tibia-clausa and vox-humana, to contrast with a stop such as the trumpet. In addition, the organ was fitted with percussion functions – drums, castanets, a vibraphone and xylophone, and a range of special effects, useful for accompanying silent films, such as a train whistle or a doorbell – the so-called 'toy counter'.

Rather than replacing the cinema organ, the coming of talkies gave the organ a new role – that of a solo presentation instrument – and the star organist was born, the console elevator lifting him or her out of the orchestra pit and into view. A peculiarly British speciality was the huge and elaborate glass console surround, which would light up and change colour automatically as the organist played.

The popularity of the organ started to wane at about the same time as cinemas began to experience the initial competition from television. Organists were among the first redundancies, by then viewed by exhibitors as dispensible. Some of the organists accepted cinema management jobs and settled for playing at children's Saturday morning matinees or in their spare time. The ABC circuit retained a team of touring organists up until the 1970s; the West End remained a bastion of organists, the last one still playing until his death in 1974. With the subdivision as well as the closure of cinemas, the majority of organs have disappeared from the cinema; most were destroyed, but some have been reinstalled in the sitting rooms of enthusiasts.

Reginald Dixon, one of the great names of the cinema organ, featured on the souvenir brochure for the Granada, Woolwich, south-east London, 1937

The great Radio Star Reginald Dixon one of Granada's Guest Organists at the console of the Mighty Wurlitzer

Music reproduced by permission of B. Feldman & Co.   Printed in England by Jackson Press (TU), London, E.13

24: The Expanding Screen, the Contracting Cinema

At the outbreak of the Second World War on 3 September 1939, all British cinemas closed, but after only a week they reopened as a popular psychological boost. Despite the raining bombs of the blitz, cinemas did well during the war with audiences flocking to escape the gloom and doom, chancing death while enjoying Betty Grable. At an impending air raid a warning would be flashed on the screen, but most audiences seemed to prefer to remain in their seats than take shelter; an option which was not open to the cinema staff. The peak wartime attendance reached a staggering 31,000,000 admissions per week. Remarkably, few cinemas were destroyed, save those lost in city-centre obliterations like that at Coventry. A number were damaged, to be patched up later, some having to wait until building restrictions were lifted in the mid 1950s. Possibly the shortest lived cinema ever was the Odeon, Canning Town, in east London. It opened in May 1939 and closed, due to bomb damage, just twenty-three months later.

Cinema building was considered inessential work and had to cease during the war. Three Odeon and three ABC schemes commenced before 1939 had to wait until the 1950s for completion. After the war, a number of Odeon projects still at the planning stage were dropped by the company, as districts were found to have changed demographically. The war deprived us of an extraordinary Odeon at Cambridge, designed by Thomas Cecil Howitt, which was to have had a tower resembling that of Stockholm town hall.

By 1949 there were 4800 cinemas and a further thirty newsreel theatres in Great Britain, the greatest number of cinemas ever in operation in this country, providing one seat for every ten of the population. It was a period when an evening at the movies seemed at its most attractive, providing as it did, an escape from the power cuts, food rationing and the shortages of austere post-war Britain. People were in the mood to enjoy themselves, and after six years of anguish they were at last able to do so. This movie heyday was not to last, for television, tentatively launched before the war and abandoned for the duration, had recommenced service in 1946. In no time at all, the 'war generation' married and settled down to family life. After the purchase of a television set, many people rarely left their homes for entertainment, bringing to an end the era of regular visits to the cinema. For many, television moved into the home for the phenomenally successful broadcasting of the Queen's Coronation of 1953, the audience able to follow the entire proceedings in their own homes.

Movies fought back with colour, panoramic screens and stereo sound effects. The desire for colour film reached back to the dawn of cinema; Robert Paul's show at the Alhambra, Leicester Square, in 1896, included tinted film, each frame laboriously painted by hand, a process which persisted until the bi-colour camera and film printing were invented in 1906 and a three-strip system in 1932 (Technicolor). Even so, colour films were still rare before the Second World War. More colour films came out of the Hollywood studios during the 1940s but the universal showing of these films was inhibited by the unwieldy bulk of the special Technicolor camera. When the simpler 'Eastman Color' process was introduced in 1950, the production of colour films rapidly increased.

Experiments to expand the size of the standard film picture (arbitrarily set at 35mm by William Dickson for the Edison Kinetoscope) had also begun before the Second World War. In the 1930s the 'Magnascope' screen was introduced, which removed the masking on a conventional screen to create a huge picture filling the proscenium, thereby increasing the dramatic impact of certain sequences. The pioneer wide-screen system was Fred Waller's 'Cinerama', the first public exhibition of which took place in New York in 1952. It was, however, by far the most cumbersome system involving three synchronised movie cameras, the process being repeated in the cinema by three projectors and a fourth film carrying seven stereophonic sound-tracks. Where the images met on the screen the edges were blurred by a sawtooth device in the projectors. The film synchronisation was controlled by an operator sitting in front of the deeply curved screen. The initial presentation, entitled 'This is Cinerama', opened with a roller-coaster ride which was so realistic that audiences experienced nausea or dizziness. The London Casino theatre in the West End was converted for Cinerama in 1954. It was exciting (as the author remembers) to experience 'This is Cinerama' here, especially when, after an introduction on the normal ratio screen by the American broadcaster Lowell Thomas, the picture enlarged to gigantic proportions, seeming to envelop the field of vision. Cinerama films were presented in key city-centre cinemas across Britain. There were just six films made using the process, the first four of which were travelogues, and it was eventually overtaken by the single-lens 70mm system.

Cinerama was too elaborate and expensive to install in every cinema, but Twentieth Century-Fox's Cinemascope, launched with a biblical piece, *The Robe*, at the Roxy in New York in 1953, became standard everywhere. This ingenious process, invented by a French professor of physics, Henri Chrétien, compressed the image, by means of the anamorphic lens, onto standard 35mm film stock and,

Cinerama technology revealed. From a brochure produced for Cinerama's London home, the Casino (now the Prince Edward Theatre), c.1955

with a corresponding lens fitted to the projector in the cinema, produced a panoramic picture. Apart from the special lens on the projectors, the exhibitor had to install a wide screen, with motorised masking at each side for adjusting the image width. There were ructions in the industry when Fox expected this to be done overnight. *The Robe* was shown at the Odeon, Leicester Square, two months after its American première. Early Fox trademark footage had the screen appearing to expand accompanied by a specially extended version of the Fox 'fanfare' music. Other Hollywood studios competed with their own improved picture systems, such as Paramount's VistaVision, and Todd-AO, a collaboration between the American film producer, Michael Todd and the American Optical Company. Three-dimensional films were short-lived, as audiences had to wear cardboard glasses handed out in the cinema in order to experience the effect, but stereo sound was easy to install, so that today most cinemas have this facility. The possibilities of presenting an audience with a gigantic colour picture and surrounding it with stereo sound encouraged film producers to come up with epics lasting many hours, and usually set in the Roman Empire. A number of this genre from the 1920s, such as *Ben Hur*, were remade at this time.

But what of new cinemas built after the war? By the end of the golden age between the two World Wars, there were as many cinemas as could be regularly filled. Some areas were over-provided and experienced overseating or 'redundancy', as it was known in the trade, and weaker cinemas, particularly those at the end of the film distribution cycle, were forced to close when the going got tough in the 1950s. The moratorium on cinema construction lasted not only through the war, but also during the following ten years, by which time we were entering the television age and many schemes were no longer required. In the meantime, the Rank Organisation (successors to the Odeon circuit) had, by 1948, acquired Gaumont-British, combining this company with Odeon to create a vast conglomerate controlling altogether 596 cinemas. Rank completed Odeon schemes at Worcester, and Westbourne Grove and Highgate in London, in 1955. T. P. Bennett and Son redesigned the auditorium of the Gaumont, Holloway (which had been badly damaged in 1944), in mundane mode, to reopen in 1958. Pre-war ABC schemes at Aberdeen, Woolwich and Gloucester were modified and reopened in 1954-6. The independent Cecil cinema at Hull, which had also been destroyed, was reconstructed on an adjacent site in 1955. But flair had flown with these buildings. Art deco was dead and they had nothing new to say; these buildings were little more than respectable brick boxes with serviceable interiors. An exception was the recast of the Broadway cinema in Birmingham into the Cinephone (by H. Werner Rosenthal, 1956), which featured an uncompromising glazed façade. Of entirely new cinemas of the post-war decade, the National Film Theatre, whose fan-shaped and stepped auditorium (designed by N. Engleback of the London County Council Architect's Department, 1956-8) nestling under the south end of London's Waterloo Bridge, was a fresh concept, both architecturally and in terms of film exhibition.

New cinemas appeared in the 1960s largely as a result of redevelopment schemes, inevitably many of them in London where development pressure is always greatest. Burnet, Tait and Lorne's fine Curzon cinema in Mayfair was sacrificed to this god. The same practice was responsible for the new Curzon built on the same site in 1966 (job architect H. G. Hammond). The ingenious planning fitted the foyer into a semi-basement below a stadium-style auditorium, above which were piled eight storeys of offices and flats. The wonderfully eccentric Regal, Marble Arch, had become an Odeon in 1945. It closed in 1964, to be replaced three years later by a new cinema incorporated into a huge office development. This new Odeon was the largest cinema to be built in London since the 1930s. However, not only did we lose the Regal's extraordinary interior but the redevelopment (designed by T. P. Bennett and Son) broke the architectural continuity of this important site facing Marble Arch. The new auditorium had to be reached by escalator, with further stairs up to the balcony, which was not ideal. But the auditorium is spacious, with an elegant curving proscenium and wall surfaces broken by textured panels backed by curtaining. The stalls floor is raked and then stepped, providing excellent conditions for viewing the giant panoramic screen – the largest in London. Head and shoulders above these developer's solutions, the one really exciting work of cinema architecture of this period was the Odeon, Elephant & Castle, London, of 1966, designed by the Hungarian architect, Ernö Goldfinger, which is dealt with on page 127.

By 1965, audiences had dwindled to such an extent that the number of operating cinemas had been more than halved – down to 1971 – from the 1949 figure. Independent operators could not compete against the large chains, and the 'barring' system, whereby non-circuit houses were excluded from showing films until they had gone the rounds of the major circuits, did not help matters. As a result, most of the independents, unless they were in a 'solo' location, gave up the fight. Of the cinemas that remained open, many were too large for the reduced audiences, and subdivision was the obvious solution. Rank launched their first twin-auditorium cinema at the Odeon (formerly the Ritz), Nottingham, in 1965. Although Verity and Beverley's fine art-deco auditorium was lost in the process, the subdivision was necessary to create a cinema complex in line with the release pattern of the day. The 1960s was the era of the 'roadshow' film, where a feature would be marketed like a theatre performance, with separate programmes, all seats bookable at higher prices than the general-release films and running at the same city-centre venue for many months, sometimes for over a year. In Nottingham, the smaller Odeon 1, seating 900, was intended for this purpose, while the larger number 2 auditorium,

Odeon, Elephant & Castle, south
London, 1966

The Odeon, Elephant & Castle, south London 1966

Architect: Ernö Goldfinger

The Odeon at Elephant & Castle was the most interesting and innovative cinema to have been built in Britain since World War Two. Its Hungarian constructivist architect, Ernö Goldfinger, was a leading modernist of the post-war era and a hero of the generation then in charge of London's civic architecture and planning.

Elephant & Castle, named after the famous hostelry on one corner of the site, is a busy intersection where streets from central London converge and then fan out again to communicate with suburban south London. In the early 1960s, with the growth of vehicular traffic, the London County Council wished to ease traffic congestion by replanning the intersection. All the buildings were compulsorily purchased, including George Coles's magnificent Trocadero cinema, then leased by Rank, which was demolished after closure in 1963. The replacement Odeon, designed by Goldfinger, which opened three years later, was built on a site slightly east of the Trocadero, the remaining area being redeveloped as an office block, also the work of Goldfinger.

The new cinema provided an opportunity for a free-standing cinema, rather than one relegated to a basement as was so often the case in redevelopment schemes of the 1960s. Goldfinger produced a 1000-seat auditorium in stadium form, with the rear seating raised above the foyer. It used the available space extremely well so that the entire ground plan of the cinema was devoted to the auditorium. A true constructivist architect, Goldfinger expressed the roof structure in his auditorium using a reinforced concrete portal beam to support the projection box in the ceiling, with two more beams radiating out towards the screen describing the projection throw. The cinema had a sculptural quality which contrasted with the adjacent blocks of offices, and varying wall textures emphasised its different components.

When the cinema opened, the shuttered concrete foyer was described as 'an extension of the pavement', which one writer suggested 'provides little opportunity for misguided and over-enthusiastic advertising'. Between the films the screen floated in a haze of coloured lights with none of the usual surrounding drapery.

The cinema passed to another operator in 1981, closing in the spring of 1988. In August that year, the owners got wind of a possible listing order on the cinema and demolition started over one weekend. The site is still vacant nearly eight years later.

seating 1450, screened general releases. The 70mm wide-screen films also required a level projection 'throw', rather than the steep-angle projection from the back of the balcony and this could be more easily achieved in these new, lower auditoria.

Naturally, this policy of subdivision was justified as providing the public with more choice, rather than what it really was: a rationalisation plan. Rank went on to subdivide most of their cinemas throughout the 1970s; the most economic way to achieve this was to drop a wall down from the balcony front, closing off the rear stalls. This area would then be partitioned down the centre to make two small studio cinemas, resulting in three auditoria in one building. From the architectural point of view, this policy was kind to interiors, as only the least interesting part of the auditorium was compromised, but operationally one ended up with disparate-sized spaces; one large auditorium comprising the balcony and front stalls area, perhaps still seating up 1000; and two small spaces of barely 200 seats each. Additionally, a ground-floor projection room had to be provided. Sometimes the former front-stalls seats would be removed as they were considered redundant.

The ABC subdivisions, starting with the former Regal, Edinburgh in 1969, tended to be more comprehensive. They extended the balcony forward to the old proscenium and divided the former stalls area unequally to gain three auditoria of diminishing size, of say, 800, 500 and 200 seats. Such schemes, of course, totally wrecked the original auditoria. Granada dabbled with subdivisions but, being a smaller exhibitor, the company saw more money in bingo and converted most of their cinemas to this use. The Classic chain, previously operators of newsreel cinemas and 'second-run houses', expanded by acquiring redundant Odeons and the old Essoldo chain – a name derived from that of its owner, Solomon Sheckman, his wife Esther and their daughter Dorothy! Most of Classic's cinemas were unattractively subdivided. The interiors of the grand West End movie palaces were systematically wrecked (see pages 50 and 106 for descriptions of the Empire and Odeon cinemas in Leicester Square), and this treatment was also meted out to the Plaza, Carlton, Warner and Rank's Leicester Square Theatre.

Odeon (formerly the Ritz), Nottingham, subdivided into two auditoria in 1965

25: The Third Age of the Cinema

In Britain we invariably follow what happens in the USA, whence the multiplex cinema originated. The multiplex consists of a number of similarly sized cinemas under one roof, attached to a single foyer and usually surrounded by acres of parking. The emergence of this new building type is symptomatic of suburban 'car culture'; with universal car ownership, the distance to a cinema is of no importance, but ease of parking is vital. Very often the multiplex in the USA formed part of a shopping 'mall'.

The multiplex was slow to catch on in Britain, where further suburban sprawl is impossible, and planners suppressed applications for green-field site shopping complexes. However, redundant ex-industrial land is ideal for this kind of development, and there is a plentiful supply of this type of acreage in the Midlands and the North of England where the multiplex has established itself easily. But the first British multiplex came about in a different way – as part of the proposed amenities of the new car-orientated city of Milton Keynes, the development corporation were keen to have a cinema. When no British exhibitor showed any interest in operating the cinema, they approached the American Multi-Cinema company, which built the Point cinema in 1985. The Point crowns the summit of a low hill, making it visible within the city, and the outer foyer block is in the form of a pyramid, hence the name. Attached to the rear of this striking architectural statement is an anonymous structure containing ten small auditoria, each one with a capacity of some 200 seats. Each unit is rectangular with straight unadorned walls. Subsequent multiplexes integrate the foyer and auditorium block.

The ABC chain commenced building the second British multiplex as part of a regeneration project for the former Manchester docks, but by the time it opened in late 1986 the company had changed hands. The MGM, Salford Quays, designed by Howard and Unick, is typical of multiplex cinemas to date, being a low industrial structure provided with a symmetrical post-modern frontage to indicate the location of the entrance. Internally, a spacious foyer leads to a series of units almost identical in their austerity. Multiplex foyers are distinctly more interesting than the auditoria, as lower land values in non-city centre sites allow for more generous circulating spaces. The foyer is also required to house fast-food outlets and movie spin-off merchandising concessions. In general, there appears to be a poverty of imagination

Point, Milton Keynes, 1985

MGM, Glasgow, Scotland, 1995

on the part of the architects involved in designing the multiplex. Some seem to take their cue from the interiors of a well-known chain of hamburger restaurants. The brash and garish lobby of the rebuilt Warner in Leicester Square is a particularly unpleasant example. A return to any kind of fake historicism would now appear tawdry and inappropriate but, for buildings largely visited by the young, some tangible atmosphere would not go amiss to accentuate the experience of an evening out, somewhat on the lines of the disco-nightclub.

At the time of writing we now have seventy-two multiplexes in Britain, many constructed by American companies (United Cinemas International, Showcase and Warner Brothers), with indigenous investment coming from Rank (with some dozen multiplexes) and ABC's successors, Cannon-MGM (eighteen multiplexes). In some instances Rank and MGM have sacrificed their existing town-centre cinema when their new multiplex has opened, such as the fine listed Cannon at Northampton. But where there is sufficient business, the old town-centre cinema and the new project have been allowed to co-exist, as at Brighton and Liverpool. American-owned multiplexes now compete within the same business park at West Thurrock, Grays, where seventeen screens divided between UCI and Warner fight for Essex man and his lady.

So successful has been the arrival of the multiplex that we are now experiencing the third great age of construction for the movies, the first being the Edwardian cinema of silent days and the second, the great era of the movie palace between the World Wars. Cinema admissions fell to an all-time low in 1984 of 54 million. Since then, however, they have climbed steadily, reaching 123·53 million in 1994, proving that Hollywood and Britain are producing popular films again and that people are regaining the film-going habit. A recent statistic stated that a staggering forty per cent of movie-goers have no set idea of which film they wish to see, which takes us back to the days of half a century ago when the medium was a kind of drug, absorbed in liberal quantities and at frequent intervals. Public reaction to the multiplex is tied to theories about ease of car parking and maximum choice of films, but we need to know what the audience thinks of the banal cinema design of today.

Reassuring design quality is present in the quaintly named Harbour Lights cinema erected in 1995 close to the site of the Cunard Ocean Terminal building in Southampton (see p.104). For this British Film Institute-sponsored initiative, the architect John Burrell has placed the foyer beneath the parallel rake of the twin auditoria. A glazed fin, housing a stair tower, asymmetrically divides the main façade. The building expresses an auditorium purpose, if not quite saying 'cinema' or even 'entertainment' – a continuing dichotomy inherent in this type of building if the architect wishes to remain within the parameters of modernist good taste. The marine jauntiness of the exterior of the Harbour Lights complements the yachts in the newly created quay, and the cinema is possibly the most notable to have come along in the last thirty years – conceivably since Goldfinger's now lost Odeon, Elephant & Castle. The building is 'architecture' in comparison to the industrial shed with Lego-Land appendages that is the average multiplex. Other architects have yet to discover a worthwhile identity for the third generation of cinema buildings.

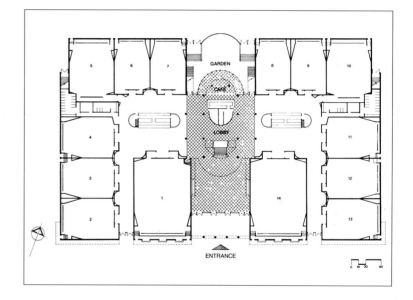

Plan of a typical multiplex cinema

Glossary of Architectural Terms

Adam style The British neo-classical style of the late-eighteenth century, evolved by Robert Adam (1728-92), which became fashionable again at the end of the nineteenth century.

Aedicule The framing of an opening by columns and a pediment.

Arabesque Surface decoration of symmetrical classical motifs, characteristic of the Italian Renaissance.

Auditorium Part of a cinema or theatre occupied by the seated audience.

Baroque architecture Originating in Italy, the European style of the seventeenth and early-eighteenth centuries, it is characterised by exuberance, curvaceousness and overscaling.

Beaux Arts style The classical style propounded by the École des Beaux Arts in Paris during the nineteenth century.

Chinoiserie A European imitation of Chinese decoration, initially fashionable during the eighteenth century.

Coffering Decoration of a ceiling or the underside of an arch, consisting of sunken squares of polygonal ornamental panels.

Cornucopia Horn of plenty; a goat's horn represented in art as overflowing with flowers, fruit and corn.

Crenellation A parapet, or battlement, with alternating indentations and raised portions.

Cupola A small dome crowning a roof or tower.

Cyclorama Curving screen placed at the rear of a stage on which scenic and atmospheric effects can be projected.

Diocletian window A semi-circular window divided into three vertical sections, originally used for Roman baths built by the Emperor Diocletian, hence the name.

Faience Originally a decorated earthenware from Faenza, Italy, which was used as a facing material for buildings from *c*.1870 up to the Second World War.

Linen-fold panelling Small-scale Tudor panelling representing linen laid in vertical folds.

Loge The French for private box, often used in theatres.

Lotus bell capitals Capitals in the shape of a water-lily, superimposed on an inverted bell formation, found in ancient Egyptian architecture.

Neo-classical architecture Originally a late-eighteenth century reaction to the excesses of the baroque style, re-establishing architecture based on Roman and Greek principles.

Œil-de-bœuf window Small round window.

Pantile A roofing tile in a curving 'S' shape.

Pediment In classical architecture, a low-pitched gable above a portico.

Pergola A garden structure of timber joists festooned with climbing plants.

Proscenium The arch framing the stage or screen and dividing these from the auditorium.

Putti Cherubs.

Regency style The decorative style prevalent during the time of the Prince Regent in the early-nineteenth century.

Rococo style A lighter, more frivolous development of the baroque style, prevalent around 1740-50.

Scarab Sacred beetle of ancient Egypt.

Swag A festoon in the form of a piece of cloth draped over two supports.

Torchère Stylised electric light fitment simulating a flaming torch.

Travertine Porous light-coloured stone, which will take a polish like marble.

Venetian window Window with a triple opening, the central one arched and wider than the others.

Statutorily Listed Cinemas: A Future for the Past?

For forty years the great and glorious movie palaces have been under attack. First from television competition, then from conversion to bingo halls (although it has to be said that the popularity of this game has saved some of the largest and finest cinemas from demolition), insensitive subdivision, and most recently from the arrival of the multiplex. Now, even bingo operators are deserting cinemas for purpose-built halls.

Not every cinema was a masterpiece of design, but it is becoming accepted that efforts should be made to retain the best and most representative examples as a constituent part of the nation's architectural heritage. The minimum protection from summary demolition is government statutory listing. Demolition of a listed building incurs a substantial fine and in practice, listing is effective in keeping cinemas standing. But there is precious little legislation to encourage the use of cinemas for the purpose of showing films, other than a government policy guideline for the control of all listed buildings which states that 'The best use will very often be the use for which the building was originally designed'. There is little that can be done to disuade an operator from closing down a cinema and either converting it to some other purpose or disposing of the property altogether. Even today, with increased audiences, independent operators sometimes cut and run when a good offer is in view. This not only amounts to a public amenity loss, which should be of concern to responsible local authorities, but where the case involves a listed and important cinema, the question of suitable re-use arises. Bingo and church use involve least alteration to the interior, but a better use would be as a performing arts venue or local meeting hall. Regrettably, so few cinemas have achieved a renewed existence through the last two uses, mainly because an earlier generation of redundant variety theatres passed into public ownership some thirty years ago, when local communities feared they might be without a theatre. Notable exceptions are at Ipswich, where the Regent cinema is now controlled by the local authority, and Horsham where a complex land deal involved the sacrifice of one cinema and the conversion of another as the core of a theatre and art gallery complex incorporating a small studio cinema. In the USA the story has been more satisfactory: while many fine cinemas have closed and been demolished, many others have been saved by local communities realising that the buildings had a further, valuable contribution to make as concert halls and as a home for touring productions of all types – popular music, theatre, opera and ballet.

Since 1992 responsibility for 'listing' in England has passed to the Department of National Heritage, who are advised by English Heritage, the government-sponsored conservation agency. In Wales, listing is carried out by CADW (part of the Welsh Office) and in Scotland, by Heritage Scotland (a division of the Scottish Office). In Northern Ireland, listing is the responsibility of the Department of the Environment. A building that is 'listed' cannot be summarily demolished without permission from the local planning authority, who will take advice from the appropriate national conservation agency. There are three grades of listing in England and Wales, I, II* and II (Grade II* indicates a building of greater quality than Grade II and is therefore eligible for a grant towards restoration). In Scotland, buildings are listed A, B and C.

A building is listed in two ways. The three national agencies operate rolling survey programmes whereby areas (usually tied to a local authority boundary) are systematically re-surveyed to find buildings of sufficient quality to be considered for listing. Alternatively, buildings can be 'spot listed', which simply means that a building can be singled out for listing when there is no re-survey programme active in that area. This can be done for speed when a building is under threat. Initiatives for spot listing can come from the national building conservation amenity groups (the Cinema Theatre Association has been remarkably effective in successfully obtaining listings for cinemas) and local authorities, but there is nothing to stop the private individual from proposing a building for listing.

In 1972, the first cinemas were listed by the Department of the Environment; they included the Granada, Tooting, the New Victoria, in central London and the Electric Palace, Harwich. In England and Wales there are no cinemas listed Grade I.

In the following list, those buildings marked * are Grade II* status. Both the original and present names are shown, together with their present use, their address, and the name of the architect where known. The lists are complete up to February 1996.

Statutorily Listed Cinemas

ENGLAND

Aldershot, Hampshire
Palace (nightclub)
Station Road, Aldershot

Bath, Avon
Forum 1934 (church/concert hall)
St James's Parade, Bath
*William Watkins and
A. Stuart Gray*

Beau Nash/Cannon 1920 (cinema)
Westgate Street, Bath
Alfred Taylor

Berkhamsted, Hertfordshire
Rex 1938 (disused)
High Street, Berkhamsted
David Nye

Beverley, East Yorkshire
Playhouse 1886 (cinema)
Market Place, Beverley
*Musgrave of Hull,
as Corn Exchange in 1886.
Cinema from 1911*

Regal 1839-48 (disused)
Manor Road, Norwood
J.H. Lockwood, as Public Hall

Birmingham, West Midlands
Odeon/Top Rank 1935 (bingo)
Kettlehouse Road, Kingstanding
J. Cecil Clavering

Blackburn, Lancashire
Exchange Hall/Apollo
1865 (cinema)
King William Street, Blackburn
*Brakspear.
Cinema from 1909*

Blackpool, Lancashire
Odeon 1939 (cinema)
Dickson Road, Blackpool
W. Calder Robson

Central King Edward 1913
(amusement arcade)
Central Drive, Blackpool

Brighton, East Sussex
Duke of Yorks 1910 (cinema)
Preston Circus, Brighton
C.E. Clayton

Broadstairs, Kent
Windsor *c.*1913 (cinema)
Harbour Street, Broadstairs

Bury, Lancashire
Art 1922 (bingo)
Knowsley Street, Bury
Albert Winstanley

Chelmsford, Essex
Regent 1916 (bingo)
Moulsham Street, Chelmsford
Francis Burdett Ward

Chester, Cheshire
Odeon 1936 (cinema)
Northgate Street, Chester
Robert Bullivant

Crewkerne, Somerset
Palace (nightclub)
West Street, Crewkerne

Esher, Surrey
Embassy/Cannon 1937 (cinema)
High Street, Esher
David Nye

Faversham, Kent
Odeon/New Royal 1936
(cinema/community centre)
Market Place, Faversham
Andrew Mather

Felling, Tyne & Wear
New Imperia 1930 (bingo)
Victoria Square, Felling

Grays, Essex
State 1938 (disused)
George Street, Grays
F.G.M. Chancellor

Great Yarmouth, Norfolk
Gem/Windmill 1908
(cinema/amusement arcade)
Marine Parade, Great Yarmouth
Arthur Hewitt

Regent 1914 (bingo)
Regent Road, Great Yarmouth
Francis Burdett Ward

Hailsham, East Sussex
Pavilion 1921 (disused)
George Street, Hailsham

Hanley, Staffordshire
Regent/Odeon 1929 (disused)
Piccadilly, Hanley
William Trent

Harrogate, North Yorkshire
Odeon 1936 (cinema)
East Parade, Harrogate
W. Calder Robson

Hartlepool, Cleveland
Majestic/Odeon 1936 (nightclub)
Raby Road, Hartlepool
W. and T.R. Milburn

Harwich, Essex
Electric Palace 1911 (cinema)
King's Quay Street, Harwich
Harold Hooper

Hull, Humberside
Tower 1914 (nightclub)
Anlaby Road, Hull
J. Percival Binks

Ilkeston, Derbyshire
Scala* 1913 (cinema)
Market Place, Derbyshire
James Parsons and Sons

Leeds, West Yorkshire
News Theatre/Classic
1938 (nightclub)
City Square, Leeds
Cecil Masey

Majestic 1922 (closed)
City Square, Leeds
Pascal J. Steinlet

Leicester, Leicestershire
Picture House 1910 (fragment)
City Hall Square, Leicester
Naylor & Sale

Liverpool, Merseyside
Forum/MGM 1931 (cinema)
Lime Street, Liverpool
*William Glen and
A. Ernest Shennan*

London

Angel 1913 (tower only, derelict)
Islington High Street, Islington
H. Courtenay Constantine

Astoria* 1930 (church)
Seven Sisters Road, Finsbury Park
Edward Stone

Astoria/Academy* 1929
(rock venue)
Stockwell Road, Brixton
Edward Stone

Avenue* 1932 (church)
Northfields Avenue, Ealing
Cecil Masey

Capitol/Jasmine 1929 (bingo)
London Road, Forest Hill
John Stanley Beard

Carlton/Mecca 1930 (bingo)
Essex Road, Islington
George Coles

Coronation 1921 (snooker)
High Street North, Manor Park
Clifford Aish

Electric* 1910 (disused)
Portobello Road, Ladbroke Grove
Gerald Seymour Valentin

Electric 1908 (shop)
Upper Street, Islington

Electric Pavilion/Ritzy
1911 (cinema)
Brixton Oval, Brixton
E.C. Homes and Lucas

Forum 1934 (dance hall)
Highgate Road, Kentish Town
John Stanley Beard

Gaumont Palace 1934 (bingo)
High Road, Wood Green
*William Edward Trent and
Ernest Tulley*

Gaumont Palace/Apollo 1932
(concert hall)
Queen Caroline Street,
Hammersmith
Robert Cromie

Gaumont State/State 1937 (bingo)
Kilburn High Road, Kilburn
George Coles

Granada/Cannon 1930 (cinema)
Hoe Street, Walthamstow
*Cecil Masey and
Theodore Komisarjevsky*

Granada/Cannon 1937 (cinema)
Sheepcote Road, Harrow
*J. Owen Bond and
Theodore Komisarjevsky*

Granada/Cannon 1939
(cinema/nightclub)
Richmond Road, Kingston
*George Coles and
Theodore Komisarjevsky*

Granada/Gala* 1931 (bingo)
Mitcham Road, Tooting
*Cecil Masey and
Theodore Komisarjevsky*

Granada/Gala 1937 (bingo)
Powis Street, Woolwich
*Cecil Masey, Reginald Uren and
Theodore Komisarjevsky*

Grange 1914 (disused)
Kilburn High Road, Kilburn
Edward Stone

Grosvenor* 1936 (nightclub)
Alexandra Avenue, Rayners Lane,
Harrow
Frederick Bromige

Maida Vale Picture House
1912 (disused)
Maida Vale
Edward Stone

New Gallery 1924 (disused)
Regent Street
Nicholas and Dixon-Spain

New Victoria/Apollo*
1930 (theatre)
Wilton Road
Ernest Wamsley Lewis

Odeon 1936 (cinema)
Fortis Green Road, Muswell Hill
George Coles

Odeon 1935 (cinema)
Great North Road, Barnet
Edgar Simmons

Odeon/Coronet 1937 (cinema)
John Wilson Street, Woolwich
George Coles

Odeon/Coronet 1936 (cinema)
Well Hall Road, Eltham
Horace Ward

Palace 1929 (market)
South Road, Southall
George Coles

Pavilion/Top Rank 1923 (bingo)
Shepherds Bush Green
Frank Verity

Plaza 1926 (cinema)
Lower Regent Street
Frank Verity

Regal 1940 (bingo)
Camberwell Road, Camberwell
Leslie Kemp

Regal 1931 (nightclub)
High Street, Uxbridge
E. Norman Bailey

Regal/Gala 1932 (bingo)
Richmond Road, Kingston
Robert Cromie

Richmond/Odeon 1930 (cinema)
Hill Street, Richmond
Julian Leathart

Troxy/Top Rank 1933 (bingo)
Commercial Road, Stepney
George Coles

West End/Rialto 1913 (disused)
Coventry Street
Horace Gilbert and
Hippolyte Blanc

Manchester, Lancashire
Apollo 1938 (concert hall)
Ardwick Green, Manchester
Peter Cummings and A.M. Irvine

Grosvenor 1912 (public house)
Oxford Road, Manchester

Longford/Top Rank
1936 (disused)
Chester Road, Stretford
Henry Elder

Margate, Kent
Dreamland 1935 (cinema/bingo)
Marine Parade, Margate
Julian Leathart

Northampton,
Northamptonshire
Savoy/Cannon 1936 (disused)
Abington Square, Northampton
William Glen

Nottingham, Nottinghamshire
Elite* 1921 (church/shops)
Market Street, Nottingham
Adamson & Kinns

Capitol 1936 (bingo)
Church Field Lane, Radford
Reginald Cooper

Oxford, Oxfordshire
Oxford/MGM 1924 (cinema)
Magdalen Street, Oxford
Frank Matcham & Co and
J.C. Leeds

Picture Palace/Ultimate Picture
Palace 1911 (cinema)
Jeune Street, Oxford
John Wilkins

Paignton, Devon
Picture House/Torbay Picture
House* c.1912 (cinema)
Torbay Road, Paignton
Attributed to Hyams and Hodgson

Portsmouth, Hampshire
Plaza/Gala 1928 (bingo)
Bradford Junction, Portsmouth

Retford, Nottinghamshire
Majestic 1927 (disused)
Coronation Street, Retford

Sale, Cheshire
Pyramid/Liberty's
1933 (nightclub)
Washway Road, Sale
Drury & Gomersall

Salford, Greater Manchester
Salford/Rex 1912 (church)
Chapel Street, Salford

Salisbury, Wiltshire
Gaumont Palace/Odeon
1931 (cinema)
New Canal, Salisbury
William Trent & Ernest Tulley

Scarborough, North Yorkshire
Odeon/Stephen Joseph
1936 (theatre)
West Borough, Scarborough
J. Cecil Clavering

Sheffield, South Yorkshire
Abbeydale 1920
(snooker/warehouse)
Abbeydale Road, Sheffield
Dixon & Stanley

Adelphi 1920 (closed)
Vicarage Road, Sheffield

Shrewsbury, Shropshire
Granada/Gala 1934 (bingo)
Castle Gates, Shrewsbury
Cecil Masey and
Theodore Komisarjevksy

Stafford, Staffordshire
Picture House 1913 (closed)
Bridge Street, Stafford
Campbell and Fairhurst

Sudbury, Suffolk
Gainsborough 1912 (nightclub)
East Street, Sudbury

Taunton, Somerset
Gaumont Palace/Top Rank
1932 (bingo)
Corporation Street, Taunton
William Benslyn

Wells, Somerset
Regal 1935 (closed)
Priory Road, Wells
Ernest Roberts

Westgate, Kent
Carlton c.1890 (cinema)
St Mildred's Road, Westgate
Built as council offices

Weston-super-Mare, Avon
Odeon 1935 (cinema)
The Centre, Weston-super-Mare
Thomas Cecil Howitt

Wisbech, Cambridgeshire
Empire 1932 (bingo)
Blackfriars Road, Wisbech
Ward and Woolnough

Worcester, Worcestershire
Northwick 1938 (music venue)
Ombersley Road, Northwick
Edmund Wilford
& John Alexander

Worthing, West Sussex
Kursaal Dome 1911 (cinema)
Marine Parade, Worthing
T.A. Allen

York, Yorkshire
Odeon 1937
Blossom Street, York
Robert Bullivant

WALES

Aberystwyth, Dyfed
Coliseum 1904
(museum/arts centre)
Terrace Road, Aberystwyth
J. Arthur Jones (as public hall)

Ammanford, Dyfed
Welfare Hall c.1935
(club/disused)
Wind Street, Ammanford
J. Owen Parry

Colwyn Bay, Clwyd
Princess 1926-32 (bingo)
Princes Drive, Colwyn Bay

Flint, Clwyd
Plaza 1938 (bingo)
Church Street, Flint
Sidney Colwyn Foulkes

Haverfordwest, Dyfed
Palace 1913 (closed)
Hill Street, Haverfordwest

Newtown, Powys
Regent 1832 (cinema)
Broad Street, Newtown
Thomas Penson
(as Flannel Exchange)

Rhyl, Clwyd
Apollo 1937 (cinema/bingo)
High Street, Rhyl
Robert Bullivant

Swansea, West Glamorgan
Carlton 1914 (shop)
Oxford Street, Swansea
Charles Tamlin Ruthen

Castle 1914 (adventure arcade)
Worcester Place, Swansea
C.S. Thomas Meager and Jones

Landore 1914 (retail use)
Neath Road, Swansea

Tenby, Dyfed
Royal Playhouse 1857 (cinema)
White Lion Street, Tenby
(as Assembly Rooms)

SCOTLAND

All cinemas listed Grade B unless
otherwise indicated

Aberdeen, Grampian
Capitol 1932 (concert hall)
Union Street, Aberdeen
A. Marshall Mackenzie

Dufftown, Banffshire
Picture House
Church Street, Dufftown

Dundee, Tayside
Playhouse (A) 1936 (tower only)
Nethergate, Dundee
Joseph Emberton

Rialto
Grays Lane, Lochee

Dunfermline, Fife
Cinema House/Robins
(cinema)
East Port, Dunfermline

Edinburgh, Lothian
Caley 1923 (nightclub)
Lothian Road, Edinburgh
J.S. Richardson and J.R. Mackay

County/George 1939 (bingo)
Bath Street, Portobello
T. Bowhill Gibson

Dominion 1938 (cinema)
Newbattle Terrace, Edinburgh
T. Bowhill Gibson

New Victoria/Odeon
1930 (cinema)
Clerk Street, Edinburgh
William Edward Trent

Playhouse 1929 (concert hall)
Leith Walk, Edinburgh
John Fairweather

Palace 1913
Constitution Street, Edinburgh

Glasgow, Strathclyde
Ascot/Odeon 1939 (disused)
Great Western Road, Anniesland
Charles McNair and Elder

Cosmo/Film Theatre
1939 (cinema)
Rose Street, Glasgow
James McKissack and
W.J. Anderson

Lyceum/County 1938 (bingo)
Govan Road, Govan
Charles McNair and Elder

Olympia/County 1910 (bingo)
Orr Street, Bridgeton
George Arthur and Sons

Salon 1913 (disused)
Vinicombe Street, Glasgow
Thomas Baird, Junior

Toledo/Cannon 1933 (cinema)
Clarkston Road, Muirend
William Beresford Inglis

Helensburgh, Dunbartonshire
La Scala (C) 1913
James Street, Helensburgh

Invergordon, Ross & Cromarty
Playhouse 1871, 1934 as cinema
High Street, Invergordon
W.C. Joass (as public hall),
Alexander Ross and Son (as cinema)

Perth, Tayside
Playhouse 1933 (cinema)
Murray Street, Perth
Alexander Catternach

NORTHERN IRELAND

Lurgan
Picture House (B)
(closed or alternative use)
Church Place, Lurgan

Supplementary List of Important Surviving Cinemas

ENGLAND

Ashford, Middlesex
Astoria 1939 (bingo)
Church Road, Ashford
F. C. Mitchell

Birmingham, West Midlands
Clifton 1938 (bingo)
Walsall Road, Great Barr
Ernest Roberts

Capitol 1925 (cinema)
Alum Rock Road, Ward End
Archibald Hurley Robinson

Blyth, Northumberland
Wallaw 1937 (cinema)
Union Street, Blyth
Percy L. Brown & Son

Bognor Regis, West Sussex
Picturedome/Cannon
1885 *(as Assembly Rooms)*
(cinema)
Canada Grove, Bognor Regis

Bolton, Greater Manchester
Odeon/Top Rank 1937 (bingo)
Ash Burner Street, Bolton
W. Calder Robson

Boston, Lincolnshire
Odeon 1937 (derelict)
South Square, Boston
Budge Reid

Regal 1932 (cinema/shops)
West Street, Boston

Bournemouth, Dorset
Moderne 1935
Winton, Bournemouth
E. de Wilde Holding

Odeon/Top Rank 1937 (bingo)
Lansdowne, Bournemouth
George Coles

Braintree, Essex
Embassy 1935 (closed)
Fairfield Road, Braintree
Leslie Kemp and Frederick Tasker

Bridgenorth, Shropshire
Majestic 1937 (cinema)
Whitburn Street, Bridgenorth

Bridgwater, Somerset
Odeon/Film Centre
1936 (cinema)
Penel Orlieu, Bridgwater
Thomas Cecil Howitt

Bristol, Avon
Odeon 1938 (cinema)
Union Street, Bristol
Thomas Cecil Howitt

Whiteladies Picture House/MGM
1921 (cinema)
Whiteladies Road, Bristol

Chatham, Kent
Ritz 1937 (bingo)
High Street, Chatham
Robert Cromie

Chesterfield, Derbyshire
Picture House/Winding Wheel
1923 (entertainment venue)
Holywell Street, Chesterfield

Chorley, Lancashire
Odeon/Gala 1938 (bingo)
Market Street, Chorley
P.J. Price

Clevedon, Avon
Curzon 1920 (cinema)
Old Church Road, Clevedon
Victor J. Cox

Colchester, Essex
Playhouse 1929 (public house)
St John's Street, Colchester

Colne, Lancashire
Central Hall *c.*1905-6 (factory)
Colne Lane, Colne

Dudley, West Midlands
Regent/Top Rank 1928 (bingo)
High Street, Dudley
William Trent

Odeon 1937 (church)
Castle Hill, Dudley
Budge Reid

Dunstable, Bedfordshire
Union/Star 1937 (bingo)
High Street North, Dunstable
Leslie Kemp

Erith, Kent
Odeon 1938 (closed)
High Street, Erith
George Coles

Exeter, Devon
Odeon 1937 (cinema)
Sidwell Street, Exeter
Robert Bullivant

Gaumont Palace/Top Rank
1932 (bingo)
North Street, Exeter
Percy Bartlett

Grays, Essex
Ritz 1940 (bingo)
Quarry Hill, Grays

Great Yarmouth, Norfolk
Empire 1911
Marine Parade, Great Yarmouth
Arthur Hewitt

Halifax, West Yorkshire
Regal/Cannon 1938 (cinema)
Ward's End, Halifax
William Glen

Hinckley, Leicestershire
Regent 1929 (bingo)
Rugby Road, Hinckley
Horace Bradley

Hollinwood, Manchester
Roxy 1937 (cinema)
Hollins Road, Hollinwood
Drury and Gomersall

Horsham, West Sussex
Ritz/Arts Centre 1936
(theatre/cinema)
North Street, Horsham
*L.H. Parsons with Frank Verity
and Samuel Beverley*

Ilkeston, Derbyshire
Ritz 1938 (bingo)
South Street, Ilkeston
Reginald Cooper

Ipswich, Suffolk
Regent 1929 (theatre)
St Helen Street, Ipswich
William Trent

Odeon/Top Rank 1936 (bingo)
Lloyds Avenue, Ipswich
George Coles

Kings Lynn, Norfolk
Majestic 1921 (cinema)
Tower Street, Kings Lynn
Carnell and White

Lancaster, Lancashire
Odeon/Cannon 1936 (cinema)
King Street, Lancaster
W. Calder Robson

Leeds, West Yorkshire
Hyde Park Picture House
1914 (cinema)
Brudenell Road, Leeds
Thomas Winn & Sons

Leicester, Leicestershire
Odeon 1938 (cinema)
Queen Street, Leicester
Robert Bullivant

Letchworth, Hertfordshire
Broadway 1936 (cinema)
Eastcheap, Letchworth
Robert Bennett

Liverpool, Merseyside
Trocadero 1922 (snooker)
Camden Street, Liverpool
Rees & Holt

Futurist 1912 (closed)
Lime Street, Liverpool

Gaumont/Top Rank 1937 (bingo)
Park Road, Princes Park, Dingle
William Trent

London

Ambassador/MGM 1932 (cinema)
Central Circus, Hendon
G.E. McLeavy

Astoria/Odeon 1930 (cinema)
Streatham High Road, Streatham
Edward Stone

Astoria 1927 (nightclub)
Charing Cross Road, West End
Edward Stone

Carlton/MGM 1927 (cinema)
Haymarket, West End
Frank Verity

Carlton/Ace 1928 (derelict)
Green Street, Upton Park
George Coles

Central Hall/Cannon
1913 (cinema)
Central Parade, Catford
Edward Stone

Curzon 1966 (cinema)
Curzon Street, Mayfair
H.G. Hammond

Dara 1909 (snooker)
Delancey Street, Camden Town

138

Dominion/Cannon 1936
(cinema/bingo)
Station Road, Harrow
Frederick Bromige

Dominion 1930 (bingo)
Buxton Road, Walthamstow
Clifford Aish

Dominion 1937 (bingo)
Acton High Street, Acton
Frederick Bromige

Empire/Coronet 1939 (derelict)
Mile End Road, Mile End
William Glen

Empire 1928 (cinema)
Leicester Square, West End
*Thomas Lamb (new auditorium,
George Coles 1962)*

Empress/Screen on the Green
1913 (cinema)
Upper Street, Islington

Forum/MGM 1934 (cinema)
Uxbridge Road, Ealing
*John Stanley Beard, A. Douglas
Clare and W.R. Bennett*

Forum/MGM 1930 (cinema)
Fulham Road, Chelsea
John Stanley Beard

Gate 1910 (cinema)
Notting Hill Gate, Notting Hill

Gaumont/Top Rank 1937 (bingo)
Bishopsford Road, Carshalton
Harry Weston

Gaumont/Odeon 1938 (cinema)
Holloway Road, Holloway
C. Howard Crane

Gaumont/Top Rank/Parkway
1937 (bingo/closed)
Parkway, Camden Town
*William Edward Trent, William
Sidney Trent and Daniel Mackay*

Granada/Gala 1937 (bingo)
St John's Hill, Clapham Junction
*Cecil Masey, H.R. Horner,
Leslie Norton and Theodore
Komisarjevsky*

Havana/Odeon 1936 (derelict)
South Street, Romford
Leslie Kemp and Frederick Tasker

Kensington/Odeon 1926 (cinema)
Kensington High Street,
Kensington
Julian Leathart

Kingsland Empire/Rio
1915/1937 (cinema)
Kingsland High Street, Dalston
*George Coles (1915), Frederick
Bromige (1937)*

Odeon 1937 (cinema)
Leicester Square, West End
*Andrew Mather, Thomas Braddock
and Harry Weedon*

Odeon 1938 (warehouse)
Balham Hill, Balham
George Coles

Odeon/Top Rank 1934 (bingo)
Upper Wickham Lane, Welling
George Coles

Odeon 1934 (shop)
Claremont Road, Surbiton
Joseph Hill

Odeon 1937 (cinema)
Finchley Road, Swiss Cottage
Basil Herring

Odeon 1935 (studio)
London Road, Isleworth
George Coles

Odeon 1936 (cinema)
High Street, Bromley
George Coles

Odeon 1967 (cinema)
Marble Arch, West End
T.P. Bennett & Son

Odeon/Boleyn 1938 (cinema)
Barking Road, East Ham
Keith Roberts

Picture House/Gaumont
1920 (nightclub)
Dalston Lane, Dalston
*Robert Cromie and
F. Edward Jones*

Picturedome/Phoenix
1910 (cinema)
High Road, East Finchley
? Birdwood

Plaza 1909 (closed)
High Street, Camden Town
Melville Seth-Ward

Pyke's Cinematograph Theatre
1911 (shop)
Brixton Hill, Brixton

Regal/Odeon 1933 (cinema)
The Broadway, Wimbledon
Robert Cromie

Regal/Cannon 1930 (cinema)
High Street, Beckenham
Robert Cromie

Regal/Cannon 1938 (cinema)
Streatham High Road, Streatham
William Glen

Rio/Odeon 1935 (cinema)
Longbridge Road, Barking
George Coles

Ritz/Coronet 1935 (cinema)
Turnpike Parade, Turnpike Lane
W.J. King

Savoy/Odeon 1934 (cinema)
Eastern Avenue, Gants Hill
George Coles

Savoy/Ace 1936 (snooker/derelict)
Stoke Newington Road,
Stoke Newington
William Glen

Warner/Warner West End
1938 (cinema)
Leicester Square, West End
*Edward Stone and Thomas
Somerford (façade only)*

Loughborough, Leicestershire
Odeon/Top Rank 1936 (bingo)
Baxtergate, Loughborough
Arthur Price

Curzon 1936 (cinema)
Cattle Market, Loughborough

Cinema 1938 (cinema)
Stanford Hall, Loughborough
Cecil Masey

Luton, Bedfordshire
Odeon/Top Rank 1938 (bingo)
Dunstable Road, Luton
Keith Roberts

Manchester, Lancashire
Paramount/Odeon 1930 (cinema)
Oxford Street, Manchester
Frank Verity

Morecambe, Lancashire
Odeon 1937 (shop)
Thornton Road, Morecambe
W. Calder Robson

**Newcastle-upon-Tyne,
Tyne & Wear**
News Theatre/BFI Tyneside
1937 (cinema)
Pilgrim Street,
Newcastle-upon-Tyne
George Bell

Jesmond Picture House 1921
Lyndhurst Avenue,
Newcastle-upon-Tyne
White & Stephenson

Nottingham, Nottinghamshire
Adelphi 1938 (bingo)
Forest Road, Bulwell
Reginald Cooper

Ritz 1936 (closed)
Burton Road, Carlton
Reginald Cooper

Pendleton, Manchester
Ambassador 1928 (closed)
Langworthy Road, Pendleton
John Knight

Peterborough, Cambridgeshire
Embassy 1937 (derelict)
Broadway, Peterborough
David Nye

Portsmouth, Hampshire
Palace 1921 (club)
Commercial Road, Portsmouth
A. E. Cogswell

Reading, Berkshire
Odeon 1937 (cinema)
Cheapside, Reading
A. P. Starkey

Redhill, Surrey
Odeon 1938 (nightclub)
Station Road, Redhill
Keith Roberts

Royston, Hertfordshire
Priory 1933 (cinema)
Priory Lane, Royston
E. B. Parkinson

Scarborough, North Yorkshire
Capitol 1928 (bingo)
Albemarle Crescent, Scarborough

Smethwick, West Midlands
Rink/Top Rank 1930 (bingo)
Windmill Lane, Smethwick
Wiliam Benslyn

Southampton, Hampshire
Harbour Lights 1995 (cinema)
Ocean Village, Southampton
John Burrell

Southend, Essex
Astoria/Odeon 1935
(cinema/shop)
Elmer Approach, Southend
Edward Stone

Stockport, Greater Manchester
Plaza/Mecca 1932 (bingo)
Mersey Square, Stockport
W. Thornley

Davenport 1937 (cinema)
Buxton Road, Davenport
Charles Hartley

Stourport-on-Severn,
Worcestershire
Electric/Haven 1904?-12
(shop/derelict)

Sunderland, Tyne & Wear
Black's Regal 1932 (bingo)
Holmeside, Sunderland
Gray and Evans

Sutton Coldfield, West Midlands
Odeon 1936 (cinema)
Birmingham Road,
Sutton Coldfield
J. Cecil Clavering

Wimborne Minster, Dorset
Tivoli 1936 (theatre/cinema)
West Borough, Wimborne Minster
E. de Wilde Holding

Wolverhampton, West Midlands
Odeon/Top Rank 1937 (bingo)
Skinner Street, Wolverhampton
P. J. Price

Woodhall Spa, Lincolnshire
Kinema in the Woods 1922
(conversion to cinema)
Coronation Road, Woodhall Spa

Worcester, Worcestershire
Odeon 1950 (cinema)
Foregate Street, Worcester
Robert Bullivant

Gaumont/Top Rank 1935 (bingo)
Foregate Street, Worcester
William Trent & Ernest Tulley

WALES

Conwy, Gwynedd
Palace 1936 (bingo)
High Street, Conwy
Sidney Colwyn Foulkes

Llanelli, Dyfed
Odeon/Entertainments Centre
1938 (music venue)
Station Road, Llanelli
P. J. Price

Llanelly (amusement arcade)
Stepney Street, Llanelli

Merthyr Tydfil, Mid Glamorgan
Castle (bingo)
High Street, Merthyr Tydfil

Newport, Gwent
Odeon 1938 (derelict)
Clarence Place, Newport
Arthur Price

Rhyl, Clwyd
Plaza 1931
(bingo/amusement arcade)
High Street, Rhyl
Sidney Colwyn Foulkes

Welshpool, Powys
Pola (cinema)
Berriew Street, Welshpool

Wrexham, Clwyd
Odeon 1937 (bingo)
Brook Street, Wrexham
Budge Reid

SCOTLAND

Aberdeen, Grampian
Regal/Cannon 1955 (cinema)
Union Street, Aberdeen
C. J. Foster

Ayr, Strathclyde
Playhouse (bingo)
Boswell Park, Ayr
John Fairweather

Campbelltown, Strathclyde
Picture House (cinema)
Hall Street, Campbelltown

Glasgow, Strathclyde
Granada 1935 (disused)
Duke Street, Glasgow
Lennox and McMath

Orient 1932 (disused)
Gallowgate, Glasgow
Albert Gardner

Regal/MGM 1929 (cinema)
Sauchiehall Street, Glasgow
Charles McNair

Riddrie/Vogue 1938 (bingo)
Cumbernauld Road, Glasgow
James McKissack

State/County 1937 (bingo)
Castlemilk Road, Kings Park
Charles McNair and Elder

Stonehouse, Strathclyde
Rex 1937 (warehouse)
Argyll Street, Stonehouse

Wishaw, Lanark
Playhouse 1940 (bingo)
Kirk Road, Wishaw
John Fairweather

Bibliography

Ackroyd, Harold, *The Dream Palaces of Liverpool*, Amber Valley Type-setting Services, 1987

Atwell, David, *Cathedrals of the Movies: A History of British Cinemas and Their Audiences*, The Architectural Press, 1980

Baacke, Rolf-Peter, *Lichtspielhausarchitektur in Deutschland*, Verlag Frölich & Kaufmann GmbH, 1982

Barnes, John, *The Beginnings of the Cinema in England*, David & Charles, 1976

Boeger, Peter, *Architektur der Lichtspieltheater in Berlin*, Verlag Willmuth Arenhövel, 1993

Clegg, Christopher and Rosemary, *The Dream Palaces of Birmingham*, published by Christopher and Rosemary Clegg, 1983

Clegg, Rosemary, *Odeon*, Mercia Cinema Society Publications Group, 1985

Coe, Brian, *The History of Movie Photography*, Ash and Grant, 1981

Draper, Christopher, *Islington's Cinemas and Film Studios*, Islington Libraries

Eyles, Allen, 'Oscar and the Odeons', *Focus on Film*, Tantivy Press, 1975

—, *ABC: The First Name in Entertainment*, Cinema Theatre Association, 1993

—, *Gaumont British Cinemas*, Cinema Theatre Association, 1996

Eyles, Allen and Skone, Keith, *London's West End Cinemas*, Keytone Publications, 1984

—, *The Cinemas of Croydon*, Keytone Publications, 1989

George, Kenneth, *'Two Sixpenies Please': Lewisham's Early Cinemas*, Lewisham Local History Society, 1987

Hall, Ben M., *The Best Remaining Seats: The Story of the Golden Age of the Movie Palace*, Bramhall House, 1961

High, David, *The First Hundred Years: The Story of the Empire, Leicester Square*, Amber Valley Typesetting Services, 1985

Hornsey, Brian, Extensive, on-going series of publications entitled *Ninety Years of Cinema in ...*, published by Brian Hornsey

Lacloche, Francis, *Architectures de Cinémas*, Editions du Moniteur, 1981

Bibliography

Mackintosh, Ian and Sell, Michael (eds), *Curtains!!! or New Life for Old Theatres*, John Offord Publications Ltd, 1982

Mander, Raymond and Mitchenson, Joe, *The Theatres of London*, New English Library, 1975

Manders, Frank, *Cinemas of Newcastle*, City of Newcastle-upon-Tyne, City Libraries and Arts, 1991

Margolies, John and Gwathmey, Emily, *Ticket to Paradise: American Movie Theaters and How We Had Fun*, Little, Brown & Company, 1991

Marriott, Paul J., *Early Oxford Picture Houses*, published by Paul J. Marriott, 1978

Mellor, Geoff J., *Picture Pioneers: The Story of the Northern Cinema 1896-1971*, Frank Graham, 1971

—, *The Cinemas of Bradford*, published by G.J. Mellor, 1983

Naylor, David, *American Picture Palaces: The Architecture of Fantasy*, Prentice Hall Press, 1981

Peart, Stephen, *The Picture House in East Anglia*, Terence Dalton Ltd, 1980

Pildas, Ave, *Movie Palaces: Survivors of an Elegant Era*, Clarkson N. Potter, Inc., 1980

Preedy, Robert E., *Leeds Cinemas Remembered*, published by Robert Preedy, 1980

Robinson, Peter H., *The Home of Beautiful Pictures: The Story of the Playhouse Cinema, Beverley*, Hutton Press, 1985

Shand, P. Morton, *Modern Theatres and Cinemas*, B.T. Batsford, 1930

Sharp, Dennis, *The Picture Palace and Other Buildings for the Movies*, Hugh Evelyn Ltd, 1969

Strachan, Christopher, *The Harwich Electric Palace*, published by Christopher Strachan, 1979

Thomas, Brendon, *The Last Picture Shows: Edinburgh*, Moorfoot Publishing, 1984

Thomson, Michael, *Silver Screen in the Silver City: A History of Cinemas in Aberdeen 1896-1987*, Aberdeen University Press, 1988

Valentine, Maggie, *The Show Starts on the Sidewalk: An Architectural History of the Movie Theatre*, Yale University Press, 1994

Ward, Richard, *In Memory of Sheffield's Cinemas*, Sheffield City Libraries, 1988

Webb, Malcolm, *Greater London's Suburban Cinemas 1946-86*, Amber Valley Typesetting Services, 1986

Williams, Ned, *Cinemas of the Black Country*, Uralia Press, 1982

Periodicals: General

Cinema Theatre Association Bulletin (bi-monthly)

Kinematograph Year Books 1914-70, British Film Institute Archives

Picture House, Cinema Theatre Association (annual)

Index